THE POWER OF
ONE MORE

GET THE POWER OF ONE MORE
BONUS BUNDLE

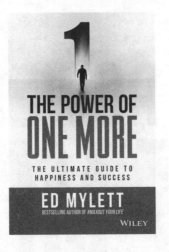

Scan the QR code or visit www.thepowerofonemore.com/bundle to get access to Ed Mylett's *The Power of One More* bonus bundle.

Tap into Ed's thoughts, actions, and strategies that will change your life forever, including:

- *The Power of One More* Chapter Guide
- Exclusive content with Ed
- How to join the Maxout community and benefit from Ed's podcasts, social media posts, and more…

THE POWER OF
ONE MORE

THE ULTIMATE GUIDE TO HAPPINESS AND SUCCESS

ED MYLETT

BESTSELLING AUTHOR OF *#MAXOUT YOUR LIFE*

WILEY

For general information on our other products and services or for technical support, please contact our Customer Care Department within the United States at (800) 762-2974, outside the United States at (317) 572-3993 or fax (317) 572-4002.

Wiley also publishes its books in a variety of electronic formats. Some content that appears in print may not be available in electronic formats. For more information about Wiley products, visit our web site at www.wiley.com.

Library of Congress Cataloging-in-Publication Data is Available:

ISBN 9781119815365 (Hardback)
ISBN 9781119815389 (ePDF)
ISBN 9781119815372 (ePub)

Cover Design and Image: Zero Degrees Media
Author Photo: © Lily Ro Photography

SKY10034684_061522

Dedicated to the man who taught me

the true meaning of One More,

my father, Edward Joseph Mylett, Jr.

Contents

THE POWER OF
ONE MORE

Introduction

THE POWER OF ONE MORE IS THE CULMINATION OF A PHILOSOPHY I've been developing for more than 30 years.

At its core, *The Power of One More* is about your willingness to do one more rep, make one more phone call, get up one hour earlier, build one more relationship, or do one more thing for whatever your situation calls for.

You can find your best life by doing "one more" than the world expects from you.

I wrote *The Power of One More* to transform your life by adopting strategies I've successfully used time and time again. By living a One More life, you can completely change your relationships, finances, emotions, the way you do business, your outlook on life, and more.

You were not born to be average or ordinary. You were born to do something great with your life. I know this about you.

The Power of One More is a dynamic contract between us. It's an important exchange of ideas and knowledge. Depending on who you are, what I'm about to teach you will impact each one of you differently. By changing how you think and act, you'll find answers in those areas of life that matter most to you.

The beauty of all this is that, most times, the answers are relatively simple.

But for whatever reasons, you may not have been able to see them or resolve them on your own. Figuring out where to begin can feel daunting. Most people are under the impression there are a thousand different things they must do to change their lives. Nothing could be further from the truth.

I've learned, and you will too, that one more thing is often all it takes. And frequently, it's only one more step away from where you are now.

Begin with ONE MORE.

You're a lot closer to changing your life than you think. **You're one more meeting, one more relationship, one more decision, one more action, or one more thought from leading the life you deserve.** *The Power of One More* **challenges you to become hyper-focused and addicted to searching for the "one mores" in your life.** The more you begin to see them and then execute the actions to realize them, the more your life will change.

The individual thoughts and actions you take don't need to be profound. However, when you compound these small thoughts and actions and stack them up on top of each other, the resulting changes over time *are* profound.

I'll teach you to keep promises to yourself, creating an internal belief system that you are destined for a better life than what you have now. When you implement One More strategies, you live by a set of principles above and beyond those of most other people.

This is not just a "how to succeed in business" or a "how to succeed in your relationships" book, although, for some, it will be. For most of you, this book will have several applications. That's why you should think of this as a **"how to succeed in your life"** book. Your challenge is to take these strategies and apply them to the areas of your life that matter to you.

There are no wasted words on these pages, but some parts of this book will connect with you more than others. Certain principles will challenge your ways of thinking, beliefs, and values. And several will land on you like a ton of bricks and change your life forever. I've purposely designed these strategies to be universal as well. You're going to read about principles that apply to *all* people in *every* area of life.

You can take lessons from each chapter whether you're a world-class athlete, a CEO, a rapidly rising star in the business world, a parent, or still in college. Some of you will use this book to transform your life completely. Others will focus on insights to enhance specific parts of your life that are lacking or troublesome.

I'm confident *The Power of One More* will resonate with you because, in many ways, I'm just like you. I'm not the person now that I was when I first started on my own transformational journey. Like you, I struggled at times. I get what it's like to worry about money, relationships, and my purpose in life. I know what it's like to lack confidence, fall into a slump, and wonder if I'll ever feel happy. I've been beyond poor, to the point I couldn't even pay the water bill in an apartment where my wife and I once lived.

I've faced health problems.

I've lost people close to me.

And over the years, **I've battled doubt, frustration, fear, and anxiety**.

I've lived with not having the answers. Even worse, I've also been in places where I didn't know what paths to take to find the answers I so desperately sought.

For those of you who have lived in a stressful or dysfunctional family, I also know what that's like. Later in this book, I'm going to tell you about the personal challenges I faced being raised by an alcoholic father who was also my hero, and how that impacted my self-esteem.

In fact, one of the reasons I've become so proficient at learning how to grow is because I had such a far place from which to come. The truth is, I needed to learn how to grow so I could simply function to reach a baseline.

The good coming from all of this is that it reinforced my belief people can dramatically change their lives. I saw it firsthand from watching how much my father changed over the years.

I also wrote *The Power of One More* because after years and years of struggling, and trial and error, I learned what it takes to succeed in life. I've paid a price, but I now know what many of the answers are and what it takes to win.

Along the way, I've also watched good friends and business associates chase what they think is fun at the expense of winning. Sadly, they become distracted and lose sight of just how good winning feels. Then they spend a lot more time and energy trying to get to a place they could have been already.

When I first started out, I often set fun aside in favor of winning. The ironic thing is, it didn't take long before I figured out that **winning *is* fun**. In fact, one of the quotes I'm best known for is, "Winning is more fun than fun is fun." When you're finished reading this book, hopefully you'll think so, too.

I've been living by these principles for 30 years, applying what I've learned to design my best life. My goal for *The Power of One More* is to help you identify your talents, gifts, and abilities, then maximize them for your own greater good and for the people around you.

Many self-improvement and performance books I read say the same thing over and over. I don't know about you, but I lose interest after a couple of chapters. I purposely set out to make *The Power of One More* different in that respect. The strategies and philosophies I'm going to share with you are unique unto themselves.

The Power of One More teaches you to combine your gifts with directed, intentional thoughts and focused actions. That gives you the resources you need to produce the standards, goals, and outcomes you deserve. Every one of the principles I share in these pages has worked for me beyond my wildest dreams. I'm also humbled and aware that I've been gifted with a certain amount of luck and God's blessings.

You have your own version of these same gifts as well. But, like me, you also need to put in the work and keep an open mind when it comes to making changes in your life. In many cases, those changes won't be easy at first. In fact, the more worthy a goal and the more changes you go through to reach it, the more resistance you'll encounter. Expect that—plan for it.

When you put yourself in the right frame of mind and you're mentally tough, you'll succeed more often than you otherwise would.

The Power of One More is the product of years upon years of how I have lived, grown, and changed my life to produce wealth, happiness, and meaningful relationships with people I care about deeply. I want to share the lessons I've learned with you so that you can lead your best life, too.

Approach *The Power of One More* like a key that will unlock your mind, and you may be surprised how **one more thought and one more action will change your life forever**.

Remember, we're a lot alike, you and me.

If I can do it, you can too.

1

One More Identity

*They always say time changes things, but you actually have to
change them yourself.*

—Andy Warhol

IN MANY WAYS, RESHAPING YOUR IDENTITY IS
THE MOST FUNDAMENTAL CONCEPT of what it
means to be a One More thinker and doer.

Your identity is a powerful and influential driver that governs
outcomes in all parts of your life. Identity defines the limits of
your success, finances, and achievements. It controls the quality
of your emotions, relationships, and self-worth.

What exactly is identity? I define it as the thoughts, concepts,
and beliefs we hold as the most genuine parts of our inner
being. You can put on a face or act a certain way for the rest of

the world, but you can't lie to yourself when it comes to these things. **Deep inside, you know what's true about you.**

Put another way, identity is this: What we perceive about ourselves is what we believe about ourselves.

Here's the paradox about identity. Many people know they could improve their lives significantly if they changed their identity. However, many people aren't willing to take the necessary steps, even when it's in their own best interests.

Are you willing to sacrifice who you are for who you could be? The answer should be a resounding "Yes!" That's a logical conclusion and sounds obvious, so it's a mystery why lots of people struggle with this fundamental question. You weren't put on this Earth to be a bump on a log, or a lump of coal in the ground. Your mission is to keep growing, expanding, and learning to lead a full and happy life. When you do these things, your identity will change.

Identity is so important because it unlocks so many other amazing things in your life. When you create a One More identity, you give yourself the gift of taking control by dictating internal messages instead of being governed by external forces that have been undermining your happiness, possibly since the day you were born.

Your Identity Is Shaped Early in Childhood

As a child, you were a blank canvas. You were impressionable, happy, and accepting.

You had no reason to believe the external world was out to hurt you in any way. Gradually, you learned to function in the world based on what you were taught by your parents, family members, friends, teachers, and others with whom you came in contact.

Of course, many people were well intentioned. However, that doesn't mean what they taught you was always right. The fact is, **nobody is ever always right**. As a child, you accepted much of what you were told, right or wrong. Your identity became the good and the bad parts of how other people influenced you. The unfortunate thing is that you were defenseless. Your critical thinking skills did not exist to give you the tools you needed to survive in the world.

As you grew older, you began to confirm your identity. If someone said you weren't a good student or a lousy athlete, that became a part of your identity. You still didn't have the capacity to disavow what you were being told. You grew into adulthood, and you carried with you these beliefs about yourself. Your identity had taken root. Your limitations became a part of you, and because they were so ingrained, you weren't even sure where they came from.

That's a lot of baggage to lug around, isn't it?

By the time you were old enough and able to question your identity, you were living with the identity you had adopted at a time when you didn't have a choice. Of course, this assumes you're even aware of how your identity impacts you. Many people simply go through life, screwed up and unsuccessful, and never quite knowing why.

However, as a One More thinker, you are now aware, and you can **change your identity once you become intentional** about it. Here's how.

Adjusting Your Identity Thermostat

I've touched briefly on your identity thermostat in the past, but now I want to give you more details on how this concept can work on your behalf.

Your identity is the force that governs your life and regulates your results. Think of it like a thermostat. **Your internal thermostat sets the conditions of your life.**

You walk into a room, and if it's too hot or too cold, you look for a thermostat to adjust the temperature to what you like. It doesn't matter what the external conditions are. The temperature can be 100 degrees outside, but if the thermostat is set for 75 degrees, it kicks on, and the air conditioning cools down the temperature and regulates the environment. The same applies when it's 30 degrees outside. The thermostat kicks in and warms your surroundings to 75 degrees.

Your life works exactly the same way. If you're a 75-degree person, you turn on the air conditioners of your life and cool it back down to what you think you're worth. This is what happens every time your results begin to exceed your identity. You unconsciously turn on the air conditioners of your life and cool it back down to what you believe you deserve.

Much like a thermostat, your identity regulates your internal self-worth. It regulates your actions and results. Many people are under the false assumption that external factors are what regulates your thermostat. They believe that getting a promotion, getting married to the love of your life, or getting an advanced degree from college determines their identity.

If you don't raise your identity, then eventually you will turn the air conditioning of your life on sooner or later, and that temperature will drop back down to 75 degrees, or some other setting you don't want, simply because you didn't take charge and decide what identity you wanted.

However, if your thermostat is set the right way, it will transcend conditions and you will find success no matter what the external conditions are.

The truth is that you can acquire all the talents, skills, and abilities you want, but until they align with your identity, you'll fall short of the goals you've set. That applies across the board.

For example, think about your fitness identity. Let's suppose you lost 20 pounds at one time in your life. Despite being armed with the best weight-loss recipes or workout regimens, a year later, you added all that weight back on and you're right where you started. That's because, when your fitness identity thermostat is set at 75 degrees, it means you're comfortable carrying 20 extra pounds, and try as you might, you'll always drift back to that 75-degree setting.

You can take all the right actions with diet and exercise, but if your internal thermostat is not set for success and remains at 75 degrees, eventually you'll drift back to your old thermostat setting by eating the wrong food or falling out of a solid workout regimen. You'll use external circumstances to find ways to cool you back down to what your internal circumstances believe you're worth.

Here's another example. Maybe you're doing well financially, but you can't seem to get to that next level of wealth you think you deserve. You may want $10 million in the bank. However, until you turn up your thermostat to believe your identity is worth $10 million, even if you make that much money, your thermostat will eventually cool you off to what your identity believes you are worth. It may take a few years, but eventually, unless you change that internal thermostat, you'll start to experience financial setbacks.

Chances are these types of situations and many others are something you've experienced.

There's no shortage of information, coaching, or paths to success in any part of your life. So it follows, the barriers to success are found inside of you. That is why you can do all the right things and still not get the results you wanted.

Remember this key point! Unconsciously, we always find a way to get back to where our thermostat is set based on what we think we're worth.

Simply put, **you can't achieve 100 degrees of fitness or wealth with a thermostat set for 75 degrees of fitness or wealth**. Your thermostat boxes you in until you can create a new identity that triggers growth and change.

This isn't to say that you can't achieve success, because you will in many cases. However, unless you adjust your identity, down the road, your thermostat will bring you back to where your identity is set.

Typically, most people blame external forces when this happens. Do these examples sound familiar?

I tweaked my back and couldn't work out for eight weeks, and then I lost interest in getting fit.

The economy turned, and I lost a ton of money in the stock market, so I gave up on my dream of being worth $10 million.

If your thermostat isn't set high enough, you'll see these as coincidences, karma, or bad luck that conspired against you. But that's not what they are. If your thermostat is set high enough, these are little more than temporary setbacks.

However, the difference between you as a One More person and everyone else is that you will view these as speedbumps on the road to your goals. **You won't use temporary setbacks as an excuse to create permanent failures.** You'll have the grit it takes to gravitate to where your thermostat is set, and eventually, you'll rise to that temperature.

Remember, as a One More person, change comes from thinking and acting. This book is not about doing one thing or the other. **You must do them in unison.** When you think and act in congruency, you don't cool your thermostat back down. Instead, you're best positioned to turn your thermostat up to achieve the results you deserve.

The Trilogy of Changing Your Identity

Once you buy into the concept that changing your identity is the key to changing your life, the question then becomes, "How do I readjust my thermostat to create my new identity?" That process is anchored in a Trilogy of core principles: faith, intentions, and associations.

Faith

According to Matthew 17:20–21, *"Truly I tell you, if you have faith as small as a mustard seed, you can say to this mountain, 'Move from here to there,' and it will move. Nothing will be impossible for you."*

Nothing moves mountains quite like faith. The same applies to moving your thermostat so that you can move your identity to a new place, too. If you're a person of faith, whether you practice Christianity, Buddhism, Hinduism, Islam, Judaism, or any other faith-based teachings, fundamentally, you believe that your God loves you.

As part of my faith, I believe that I come from the most extraordinary DNA in the world: God's DNA. As an extension of this, I also believe that God did not make me in His image to live with a thermostat set at 75 degrees. My God, and your spiritual deity, too, created us to live a full faith-based life with a thermostat set at 100 degrees.

Many people say they lead faith-based lives, but how many of us say they have God and faith in all parts of their lives? Several people I know read the Bible, go to church, and are kind-hearted and loving people. But do these same people extend their faith into their beliefs about personal fitness, finance, relationships, and business? In many cases, the answer is "No."

One of the keys to changing your identity is to let faith move mountains in *all* parts of your life.

Intentions

When our actions are based on good intentions, our soul has no regrets.

—*Anthony Douglas Williams*

I meet many people who constantly beat themselves up for where they are in life instead of giving themselves credit for their intentions to move to a new identity. If this sounds like you, all you're doing is reinforcing your current identity—your 75-degree life.

Do these moans sound familiar?

I'd give myself more credit if I had gotten that promotion.

My life is a complete mess since I got divorced three years ago.

I'm a failure since I had to claim bankruptcy during the pandemic.

You're not letting yourself up off the mat when you do this. It's a dead-bang loser of an approach to life. You're not being fair to the person who matters most—you!

Thinking this way creates a downward spiral, and the farther down you spin, the harder it is to climb out of it and create a new identity. You'll accept frustration. You won't want to be around people. And, quite frankly, most people won't want to be around you.

Instead of souring on life, **flip your script**. Tell yourself you intend to do good and to serve. That you intend to create a thriving business and have money in the bank. You intend to treat the people around you with care and are worthy of a loving and caring relationship. **Apply good intentions to all parts of your life, and then watch what happens.**

Your intentions will set your mind to work creating your new identity. **Your brain works on what it is told.** When you tell your brain what you want to attract, it will design internal messages that will feed the good parts of who you are and manifest themselves in a new identity over time. Intentions are the currency that lets you make deposits in your "identity bank" instead of you creating a run on that bank that will eventually drive you into identity bankruptcy.

Associations

Consider the words of T. F. Hodge, *"What surrounds us is what is within us."*

You can't possibly stay at 75 degrees if you hang out with people operating at 100 degrees.

Through proximity, you absorb the traits, actions, and beliefs of the people you associate with. Consciously and unconsciously, their knowledge and ideas become a part of who you are.

This is why you should seek out quality associations that can either directly or indirectly help you grow to be the 100-degree person you're meant to be.

The other side of this is that if you want to raise your thermostat and change your identity, you may need to say goodbye to many of the 50-degree people in your life.

Yes, I know that can be a hard thing to do. **Until you clear out space in your life for the right associations, you'll be mired in relationships that have outlived their purpose and now hold you back.** I'm not saying this part is easy, but at times, it is necessary.

The other way to approach this is to **reject 50-degree behavior and raise other people's thermostats** instead. This is an especially viable approach when you're dealing with family members or lifelong friends where saying goodbye could be difficult.

The bottom line is that you're a reflection of the people you associate with. If you associate with people who elevate you and make your thermostat rise, then you're on the right path to creating a new identity.

Once you're armed with awareness of the Trilogy, you can only move forward if you adjust the level of self-confidence you have to change your identity.

Self-Confidence Is the Unifying Factor

I go into greater detail in Chapter 12 on habits, but self-confidence and how it relates to identity are crucial concepts worth repeating.

The first thing to know is that **identity is different than self-confidence**. Identity is what you believe you're worth. Your internal thermostat. Self-confidence is the means to deliver on it.

Self-confident people share one habit in common, and that is **the ability to keep the promises they make to themselves**. When you're in the habit of keeping promises you make with yourself, you're on the pathway to self-confidence.

Self-confidence is also a form of **self-trust**, and if you can't trust yourself, you need to do some hard thinking about your life.

It also follows that if you're timid, you won't act. If you have doubts, you'll paralyze yourself with fear. **Doubts are the products of external factors in your life**. They are incubators for negative thoughts. When these negative thoughts grow, they take over *all* your thoughts, and your mind descends into unproductive and damaging places.

That's why you must **guard your thoughts**. Pull out the mental weeds that threaten to take over the good parts of your psyche. You may not get them all, and that's okay. Self-confidence is not about doing away with fear or timidity. It's about moving forward anyway because of the agreements you made with yourself.

The other critical thing is that **self-confidence is generated from within**. And because it's an internal emotion, you can stack the deck in your favor.

Ralph Waldo Emerson put it this way: *"What lies behind you and what lies in front of you pales in comparison to what lies inside of you."*

Let this sink in. **You are the only one who gets a say in how much self-confidence you want. When you break internal agreements, you're only fighting with yourself.** If this sounds a bit crazy, that's because it is. Wouldn't you rather save your energy for the other battles you're fighting?

Like most things in life, when keeping a promise to yourself, **the first step is always the hardest.** I guarantee that once your train of thought pulls out of that station in your head, you'll find the momentum you need to act. You'll see results as you develop a new identity. Those results will be the fuel that keeps that train moving on down the tracks.

The opposite of self-confidence is self-sabotage. It's like a computer virus that lurks inside many people and is only triggered when you try to move forward with an important part of your life. Self-sabotage triggers discouragement and doubt, the mortal enemies of self-confidence.

Farnham Street Media founder Shane Parrish perfectly described how these things could damage you when he said, *"Optimism might not make you successful, but pessimism will ensure you don't succeed."* **When you self-sabotage, you dial down**

your thermostat and deny yourself the bliss that was headed into your life.

Maybe this is you. Perhaps it's somebody you know. Some people just have a knack for being given a gift and then finding a way to undermine the outcome. The worst part is that the same people seem to repeat this type of thing over and over. They're labeled the "hot-mess" or somebody who hasn't gotten their life together yet. In reality, **they've just dialed their thermostat to what they believe they're worthy of receiving.**

How often have you seen somebody you know meet the woman or the man of their dreams, only to cheat on them, be gross and inappropriate, or downright rude? Do you know people who have made a pile of money but then go on a self-destructive spree using drugs and alcohol, recklessly spending, or gambling their wealth away? Most of us have also heard cautionary tales of pro athletes who don't train or eat well or who overindulge in vices, and in some cases, it costs them their lives. **They're all guilty of self-sabotage because their lack of discipline is a lack of self-confidence that does not match up and support their identity.** Their internal thermostat doesn't match the initial success they've enjoyed. Eventually, that thermostat resets itself, and the person crashes back down to where their thermostat says they should be.

It's sad when this happens because it doesn't need to be this way.

Here's an exercise I use to destroy self-sabotage, discouragement, and doubt. I pay attention when I have a self-sabotaging thought. I mentally record that thought. Then, I visualize and see myself scratching it out. The first time

I record the thought and strike it out, I'll still see it. So I do this repeatedly, as many times as it takes, until I can no longer see the thought because it is so marked over and blacked out. When I get to the point where I can't see it, the thought has been stricken from my mind. My mind no longer lives with the thought, and **that thought loses its limiting power on me**.

To successfully align with your One More Identity, you must keep the right promises with yourself. You must eliminate negatives and create an environment where self-confidence becomes an asset instead of one more thing you fear.

Now that you know more about how self-confidence and identity work together, it's time to look at misconceptions that can skew proper thinking.

Misconceptions About Self-Confidence and Identity

Recognize and reject these misconceptions, and you'll fortify your quest for a new identity:

- **I am what I possess.** Lots of people link self-confidence and identity to their possessions. They make the flawed assumption that the more possessions they acquire, the higher their self-confidence will be, and the more perfect their new identity will be.

    That's not the case. It's a hollow approach to self-confidence and identity.

    There's absolutely nothing wrong with acquiring material things. I would be disingenuous if I told you that. What I don't do is link my possessions and material wealth with my self-confidence and my identity. I consciously keep them separate, and so should you.

- **I am my accomplishments.** This is a horrible trap to fall into because all your life, to feel good about your self-confidence and your identity, you're going to have an insatiable need to keep accomplishing things.

  Keep it simple. You are you. You were put on this Earth to do great things but **feeding your ego is an insidious trap**. By all means, attempt great things. Accomplish great things. Just don't get so caught up in patting yourself on the back that you lose the humility you should have. Remember, it can all be taken away in an instant. And if you use your accomplishments as a crutch for your self-worth, that fall will be hard, I guarantee you.

- **I am what other people say I am.** Wrong. The essence of self-confidence and internalizing your search for a new identity flies in the face of this belief. Forget the ego strokes. Don't base your worth on social media hearts and likes. Don't beg for compliments. It's a cheap and needy way to live your life. When you do, you're doing the opposite of improving your self-confidence and designing your new identity.

- **What I look like means everything.** So many people fall into the trap of what they think beauty should be. This is especially true for women who are bombarded with television programs, blogs, podcasts, social media, and magazines, all of which place an extreme focus on external beauty.

  Here's the real deal. **True beauty comes from within**. Your beauty comes from your soul, intentions, your capacity to give, how you treat people, your beliefs, and your kind heart. It's not bad to work on your health, lose weight, dress in nice clothes, and pay attention to your grooming. The trick is to **do it for you and nobody else**. Remember, you are defined by the content of your character and not by the reflection in your bathroom mirror.

As a One More thinker, your identity is foundational to who you are. Use the Trilogy and apply self-confidence to find the right temperature on your identity thermostat. When you do, you're well on your way not only to creating your best identity but also to leading your best life.

2

One More and Living in Your Matrix

*This is your last chance. After this, there is no turning back.
You take the blue pill—the story ends, you wake up in your bed
and believe whatever you want to believe. You take the red
pill—you stay in Wonderland, and I show you how deep the
rabbit-hole goes.*

—Morpheus, The Matrix

I'**M A HUGE FAN OF *THE MATRIX*.** Not only was it a groundbreaking movie when it was released in 1999, but the film is also stacked with One More lessons. If you haven't seen *The Matrix* yet, stay with me. It's all going to make sense in a moment. Also, be advised, spoilers are ahead.

The Matrix tells the story of Keanu Reeves's character, a computer programmer, Thomas A. Anderson, who leads a double life as the hacker Neo. He joins forces with legendary hacker Morpheus in a quest to destroy artificial intelligence that is running human life, known as the Matrix. As they battle the Agents that protect the Matrix, Neo begins to display super-human gifts—including the ability to slow down time—that indicate he could be The One, or the chosen person to bring down the Matrix.

Speaking of **The One**, I want you to realize something. When you see a happy or financially successful family, understand that at some point in their history, they weren't happy or successful. That is, until **The One** showed up, and **The One** in that family changed the family tree forever.

The One can change the emotions, finances, level of happiness, and the way the family thinks, among many other things.

In my family, I am **The One**. Not because I wanted it or I liked it, but because I was ready to fight for it, and because I learned the strategies it takes to be **The One**.

My prayer for you is for you to become The One in your family.

The reason I love the story of Neo being The One is because I believe it's a metaphor for what exists in every family.

It bears repeating. When you see a family that is happy, successful, or living out their dreams, understand that they did not start out that way. And then, **The One** in that family stepped up and changed that family legacy forever.

I'm teaching you about the Matrix so that you can be **The One** who steps up in your family, too.

Here's something that may surprise you.

What if I told you that you're already living in your Matrix?

What if I told you there are already forces at work deep inside you that are slowing down parts of your life, interpreting and reinforcing what you've already programmed into your consciousness? You're not even aware this is happening.

But it is.

Your Matrix is a more colloquial name for your **reticular activating system**, RAS for short. Your RAS is the filter that gives weight to the important things in your life and filters out the things that are not.

The RAS is a concept I've talked about in the past. Much like creating a One More identity, I haven't explored it as much as we're going to do in this chapter. And just like a One More identity, learning about your RAS is vital to linking with many of the other chapters in this book.

However, while understanding the science behind your RAS is important, because people are sometimes intimidated or turned off by heavy duty scientific concepts, I've translated our discussion into a more accessible and digestible strategy using the Matrix as an example.

Whether you identify it as your RAS or your Matrix, remember this.

Think of the RAS as the filter that reveals to you what's most important to you in your life.

Here's an example that illustrates how the RAS works. Let's say you want to buy a blue van. Immediately, you start seeing blue vans everywhere. It could three lanes over on a freeway, when you're out running errands, or dropping your kids off at school.

Guess what? Those blue vans were always there, you just never noticed them before. But now you see them because they've become a part of your RAS. They have been filtered into your consciousness since they have become important to you.

This extends out to other parts of your life. For example, the clients, your level of fitness, the relationships, or the emotions you want become your blue vans. They were always there; you just never saw them because they weren't programmed into your RAS. You just filtered them out because they weren't important enough to you at the time.

How do they become important? Through repeated visualization and thought. These things teach your RAS what it should be hearing, looking for, and feeling because your mind moves toward what it is most familiar with.

This is what I mean by slowing down. When you repeatedly visualize and obsessively think about something, you tell your RAS to pay attention to that thought, and that's when the world slows down.

That's how the RAS works.

You already do this exceptionally well, but chances are you don't do it with enough direction, intention, or awareness. However, if you can direct your RAS to focus better on the blue vans in your life, then your life begins to change.

One More thinkers learn to work in concert with their Matrix. In turn, this repeatedly creates opportunities and outcomes that will fast-forward your life in countless ways.

Living a Deeper Life by Slowing Down Your Matrix

The concept of slowing down time can be traced back to ancient civilizations. The fifth-century BC philosopher Zeno posed the question, *"If a flying arrow appears to be at rest in any particular instant in flight, doesn't that actually make it motionless?"* It was one of many paradoxes he posed in his time.

We've come a long way since then. But the concept of our relationship with time still fascinates us. Just like in *The Matrix*, if you want to live a deeper, more meaningful life, you must learn to slow down your internal pace.

From a technical standpoint, *The Matrix* used cinematic special effects to create what has become known as **bullet time**. Bullet time was created by placing 120 cameras in a 360-degree circle around the action, taking thousands of shots, and then stitching those shots together. The results make viewers feel like they're moving around a slow-motion scene that plays out in a matter of seconds, which is what you ultimately see in the movie.

As directors, the Wachowskis weren't the first to use the technique, but they were the first to take it mainstream. It's used several times in *The Matrix* and subsequent sequels, but the best known and remembered use is when Neo dodges bullet after bullet on a rooftop—hence, bullet time.

Bullet time can work for you, too. It's the equivalent of an extreme version of "stopping to smell the roses." But it's a lot more than that. **When you strategically slow down your physical and mental being, you create a space that allows your senses and brain to reset.** You see things differently, and you start to realize One Mores have been there all along. You just needed to change the variables in your life to see them.

The key is to be aware of your circumstances and your environment. Bullet time allows you to go looking for one more business deal, concentrate on one more way to improve your tennis game, or one more way to make your marriage better.

I'm trying to free your mind, Neo. But I can only show you the door. You're the one that has to walk through it.

—Morpheus

It takes time and focus to engage in your present life. Much like *The Matrix*, you'll be more invested in what happens to you when you put forth this effort.

Just as important, **you must consciously decide which path you want to choose.** This brings us to the famous blue pill versus red pill choice Neo must make. When Morpheus asks Neo to choose between the pills, he essentially asks Neo to choose between fate and free will.

In *The Matrix*, taking the blue pill represents choosing fate. All choices are already decided, and actions are predetermined. The concept of choice is only an illusion. Neo instead opts for the red pill and places himself in a place of free will where he can change his fate based on his decisions. He joins Morpheus and Trinity, another key freedom fighter, who also place a higher value on free will, no matter how unpleasant that world is.

Everyone has this same ability to choose their reality. One More thinkers are simply more intentional about it. They choose free will and action because they know what they want and combine thinking and action to move them closer to their standards and goals. They raise their awareness levels. In doing so, they slow down their world. And their world changes to better align with what they want in life.

Neo, sooner or later you're going to realize, just as I did, there's a difference between knowing the path and walking the path.

—Morpheus

Because of the pace of our lives, we often choose to look at only certain things. To travel along pre-established paths. For many, it's a matter of expediency. But it also eliminates several colors in the big, beautiful rainbow of life.

Don't be too hard on yourself if this sounds like you. From the time we're born, we're taught to obey others, follow the rules, and memorize facts. As the world goes faster and faster, it's more of a struggle to keep up in a light-speed technologically driven era. To survive, we constantly accept that others decide what's best for us and that we should follow without question.

What if you challenged that assumption? Not all the time, but in the areas of your life that are important to you. What if you gave yourself a mental time-out and thought long and hard about the choices you face? **What if you explored your options more deeply when it mattered?**

One More thinkers should be more deeply engaged in their own lives when possible. Your Matrix and your choice between the red pill and the blue pill are waiting for you.

How Your Matrix Works

It's cool to attach a movie label to one of your core functions. But to fully appreciate how your Matrix works, you need to understand the science behind your Matrix as well.

I mentioned the reticular activating system (RAS) earlier. It's the mental muscle that allows you to recalibrate your Matrix.

Your RAS filters things into your awareness that are important to you and filters out the things that are not.

In neurological terms, reticular means "net or web-like." The RAS is a network web formation of nerve cells and their connections located deep in your brainstem, between your spinal cord, traversing up through your thalamus in the center of your brain. These cells extend outward to your cerebral cortex, which is the thin layer of neural tissue on the surface of your brain.

The RAS does not interpret the quality or the type of sensory input you provide it. The RAS activates your entire cerebral cortex, putting it on high alert. This increased arousal creates an enhanced ability to interpret incoming information and preps the brain for appropriate action.

Appropriate action means that the RAS alters your brain's electrical activity, regulating the electrical voltage of brain waves and the speed at which nerve cells engage. It also releases chemicals that regulate sleep, pain, motor function, emotions, and memories. These chemicals include acetylcholine that regulates movement, and dopamine, norepinephrine, and serotonin that are associated with consciousness and feelings. The RAS has been linked to psychological disorders, too. Abnormalities in the RAS result in schizophrenia, Parkinson's disease, and post-traumatic stress disorder (PTSD), among others.

When you're awake, your brain produces low-voltage brain waves that are incredibly fast so that you can organize information quickly and attentively. The same thing occurs during the rapid eye movement (REM) cycle of sleep, which produces intense dreaming, body movements, and faster breathing and pulse rates.

How the RAS configures these signals also makes you more or less alert, more or less cognizant, and will determine how your brain interprets various messages you receive. In this way, **the RAS is your brain's natural filtering system**. It filters out everything that's not important to you or unnecessary noise that interferes with your decision-making process, including processing messages when you sleep.

The RAS also filters in all the things that are important to you into your consciousness. By doing so, you can create your own reality. But you have to be intentional and work at it. For One More thinkers, your RAS is your Matrix. Understanding the science behind how your Matrix works makes it easier to understand how and why you should find ways to put it to work in your favor.

Here's a quick illustration. If you're looking for things to be offended by, your RAS will activate, and that's what you'll find all day long. On the other hand, if you're looking for things to be grateful for, that's what you'll find instead.

When you intentionally activate your Matrix to focus on certain things, you'll see One Mores everywhere.

Without consciously knowing it, your Matrix sifts through a mountain of data and presents only the pieces that are important to you. Your Matrix programs itself to work in your favor. You've heard of the saying, "garbage in, garbage out"? I'll bet you didn't know there was a whole branch of science connected to it. It's all about you and your Matrix.

Your Matrix also seeks information that validates your beliefs. It filters the world through the parameters you give it. Your beliefs shape those parameters in a self-fulfilling prophecy of sorts. If you think you're bad at hitting a golf ball, or painting as a hobby, or giving a speech, then you probably will be horrendous at those activities. Conversely, if you think you can hit a 90-m.p.h. fastball, learn a new language in three months, or master ballroom dancing in a year, you have a much better chance of doing so. **Your Matrix helps you see what you want to see, and then it goes to work to influence your actions.**

Your RAS also helps explain the Law of Attraction. This is the concept that you attract what you tend to think about. It's often touted in some kind of New Age, cosmic way, but the Law of Attraction is a lot less magical and mystical once you understand how your Matrix works.

Here's a One More thinker key takeaway. **When you can train your Matrix to take your subconscious thoughts and marry them to your consciousness, you become intentional.** I talk a lot about being intentional, and now you know how and why the process works.

It requires focus and patience. However, if you can master this skill, your Matrix will align with you to reveal information, people, and opportunities to help you achieve your standards and goals.

Training Your Matrix to Get What You Want

The next and most obvious question then becomes, "How do I train my Matrix to get what I want?" There are simple and concrete ways to do this.

You start by planting a seed in your Matrix. Think about a situation you want to influence. For example, "I want to lose weight." Next, give more directed thought to the specific outcome you want. In this case, "I want to lose 20 pounds over the next six months." Finally, start creating visualizations of how you ideally want that goal to play out. Let your imagination hear the conversations, actions, exercise, foods, and other details you'll need to reach that goal. To lock in your Matrix, you'll need to replay these things over and over with intention.

When you do this, you're unleashing your Matrix to go to work for you. **One More thinkers must also put actions to these thoughts.** It's not enough to mentally convince yourself. You can't wish your way to success.

Let's say you want a dog. You love huskies, but you never noticed how many of them you see during your day until you set your mind to work, deciding that's the kind of dog you want. Suddenly, you see huskies everywhere.

How about your dream car? Maybe all your life, you've dreamed of owning a Porsche. It's one of those "someday" dreams with no actual timetable in place. Then, your career takes off. You get a big raise and your "someday" Porsche dream starts to become real. You see online ads, TV commercials, and billboards for Porsches. Every time one passes you on the freeway, your brain fires off. You have a chance meeting with a guy who already drives a Porsche, and your Matrix elevates your dream to an even higher state.

When these things happen, your Matrix has taken the first steps in moving you closer to what you want out of life.

Your Matrix and Confirmation Bias

Confirmation bias is the tendency to interpret new evidence as the confirmation of your existing beliefs or theories. **Your Matrix and confirmation bias are joined at the hip.** When your Matrix generates specific beliefs or outcomes, confirmation bias kicks in and reinforces those beliefs, further strengthening the effect. As this happens, any evidence or theories that undermine or could disprove what your Matrix believes are undervalued.

Confirmation bias is an extension of selective recall. When you choose to remember things in a certain way that confirms what you're thinking, you'll be biased to the outcome you want to achieve. **The stronger your beliefs, or the more emotionally charged an issue is to you, the stronger your confirmation bias and selective recall will be.**

These embedded beliefs become stronger over time. Subconsciously, through repetition, your obsessions eventually become your possessions. When combined with intentional actions, confirmation bias, and selective recall, your Matrix drives you unrelentingly toward your goals. The key is to make sure the right seeds are planted in your Matrix. If you plant the wrong things, you'll harvest the wrong results.

Biased interpretations and memories can be powerful tools when you harness them the right way. In our respective worlds, we're inundated with confirmations daily. Social media is a prime example of an echo chamber that reinforces our beliefs. We gravitate toward what aligns with our thoughts and beliefs. And we often repel points of view that differ from our own.

In recent years, the media has become an obvious example of confirmation bias. Fox News, CNN, MSNBC, and others routinely express points of view that either confirm or enrage viewers, based on their political leanings.

Confirmation bias also minimizes a mental conflict known as cognitive dissonance. That occurs when a person is exposed to two contradictory beliefs, resulting in psychological stress or uneasiness. Confirmation bias helps avoid incongruent points of

view and strengthens information-reinforcing views that align
with what we want to believe.

Your Matrix Is Unique to You

Every person's Matrix is unique. Just as no two brains are alike,
the same holds true for your Matrix as well. You are the one-of-
a-kind total of your memories, experiences, thoughts,
relationships, fears, ambitions, and more. That's why **learning
how to control your Matrix is a solo journey**. You can't
delegate this responsibility. It's up to you, and only you. And
keep in mind, confirmation bias heavily influences how your
Matrix behaves.

Consider this. A Wall Street stockbroker has configured their
Matrix to find money in the vast array of financial markets. By
slowing down and letting their Matrix see opportunities, they
see deals that someone who is not intentionally wired does not.

Likewise, ponder the plight of a homeless drug addict on Skid
Row. Even though they have no place to sleep and wonder
where their next meal is coming from, they always find a way to
get their next high. They've trained their Matrix to find drugs.
And they become very good at doing it.

Both are living their realities. They have trained their Matrix
to elevate specific thoughts and opportunities consistent with
their goals, and everything they run across tends to confirm that
they're moving toward those goals. In each case, their
obsessions become their possessions. Society may judge them
differently. But is either right or wrong, or are they the result of
how their Matrix impacted their lives?

The point I make is that your Matrix is yours, and yours
alone. You control it, whether you're looking for your next big

sleeper stock or a dime bag of heroin. **And the longer your Matrix sees things a certain way, the more ingrained and intense your beliefs become.**

Here's another example. If you're a quarterback, does it make more sense in a game to avoid receivers who are covered or look for receivers who are open? When you train your mind to look for an open receiver, that's what your brain looks for instead of focusing on covered receivers.

Rookie quarterbacks often struggle because they don't have the depth of experience planted in their Matrix. But seasoned Hall of Fame quarterbacks like Joe Montana or Peyton Manning literally picked apart defenses. They were more deeply invested and embedded into believing they could control the action on the field because their world had slowed down and put them into their in-game Matrix.

It's also how an experienced color analyst in the booth like Tony Romo or Troy Aikman can spot a blitz, know what routes receivers are going to run, and what the coverage will be even before the snap of the ball. Years of experience on the field now translates into interpreting, in advance, what's going to happen on the field for millions of viewers at a time.

If you're a golfer, you filter out sand traps, water hazards, and out-of-bounds markers on every swing. You know exactly where you want to place the ball on every shot, and that's all your Matrix allows you to see.

Using your Matrix also extends to your relationships. When you activate your Matrix, you begin to see the qualities in people you want to have a relationship with instead of missing those people who were there all along.

What if, instead of huskies, Porsches, and pass routes, you focused on creating more business prospects? You would begin to hear opportunities at work or on a sales call that you wouldn't otherwise because your brain is now actively looking for these kinds of possibilities. You begin to see money-making opportunities that were always there but weren't filtered into your Matrix before.

If you're an entrepreneur, you already train your brain to look for opportunities, not roadblocks. You seek ways to connect two disparate services, products, or relationships in a way that will make you money. To some degree, your Matrix filters out all the people who are not good candidates for you to work with and instead focuses on the ones you are most compatible with.

Think about what could happen if you became even more focused on this. Would the quality and quantity of your deals rise? Would you put more money in your pocket at the end of the year? Based on my experience, yes, you would.

I'm a big believer that **everything you need is already in and around you right now** if you can just put in the work to see it.

Optimizing Your Matrix

Your Matrix is already hard at work. But is it working the right way on your behalf? Do you think about the things that will enhance your life, or are you thinking about avoiding bad things that will detract from your life? There is a difference.

Shifting your Matrix mindset to a more positive framework removes fear and anxiety and replaces those thoughts with confidence and forward momentum. To do this, two things are essential.

First, you must **intentionally elevate the quality of your thoughts**. Frame them in the positive. Set your goals so that when you achieve them, you'll be excited about the outcome instead of breathing a sigh of relief that you avoided a crisis.

Second, **repeat, repeat, repeat!**

You must continuously and consciously fill your Matrix with the thoughts you want. Let your beliefs become so embedded that you're not even aware they exist. However, your Matrix won't lose sight of them. In its way, your Matrix will become your biggest ally and turn your thoughts into results. Program your Matrix through intentional repetitious feelings, words, and visualizations. Be doggedly persistent if you want success.

Breaking it down further, activation also comes from preparation, gathering knowledge, courage, permitting yourself to fail, giving yourself permission to chart your path, gratitude, and more. Also, **remove procrastination from your life**. As Victor Kiam, an entrepreneur and former owner of the New England Patriots, said, "*Procrastination is opportunity's assassin.*" Conversely, **change is the instigator of opportunity**.

When it's time to dance with a pretty girl, you can't sit on the sidelines, otherwise, another guy will be two-steppin' with her in no time. And you'll just be left at the bar, grumpy and drunk.

Few things are more expensive than opportunities you miss. You pay for them with regret, doubt, and a lingering, haunting feeling of what could have been.

English philosopher Francis Bacon once said, "*A wise man will make more opportunities than he finds.*"

In the same way, One More thinkers are intentional about opportunities. They set their Matrix in motion and hone this powerful tool through repetition.

When you activate your Matrix, you'll bend reality and find One More opportunities that will reveal themselves to you in ways you would never have seen otherwise.

3

One More Try

It ain't over 'til it's over.

—*Yogi Berra*

IF YOU EVER WANT TO ACHIEVE ANYTHING
MEANINGFUL IN YOUR LIFE, the strategy you must
master is One More Try.

Here's why.

One More Try doesn't run in an isolated path in your life. It's
an overarching concept that links to many of the other
strategies in this book.

One of the core beliefs I hold is the importance of **compounding**.
Compounding takes place when you attempt One More Try, time
and time again. When you're successful in implementing a One More
Try mentality, you'll create and compound more wins for yourself.

Each of those wins creates an incremental advancement toward your goals. **You stack them on top of each other to produce significant long-term changes in your life.**

Here's a simple example that illustrates the point. When you were a child, the first time you tried to ride a bicycle, you didn't do so well, did you? You probably started with training wheels, going slow, and with your mom or your dad by your side to steady you.

As you climbed on your bike day after day, you got better at learning how to balance, pedal, and go forward. Eventually, those training wheels came off, and slowly but surely you started to ride away on your own. Not long after that, you were whizzing up and down streets and sidewalks without a care in the world. And your life had changed forever.

Until you understand and embrace the fundamental, life-changing power of One More Try, you won't fully understand why it's essential to try and make one more call, do one more set in the gym, meet one more person at a convention, or learn one more skill to put you head and shoulders above everyone else.

When you act and do the same things as everyone else, you'll get the same results as everyone else. When you implement a One More Try mentality, that's where you'll find your greatest successes and your most significant personal growth.

Doing so also will give you more **confidence** than your competitors. It's a secret weapon of sorts. Although they may not see it, you'll know you're willing to do more than them. You're eager to make One More Try than they are. That's a tremendous advantage in your favor.

This isn't exactly a new idea. Confucius understood the battles that go on in a person's mind when he wrote,

"The man who thinks he can and the man who thinks he can't are both right."

Confucius knew that an individual executes to the level of what he or she believes in themselves. Confidence fuels your belief that you're worthy of making One More Try.

Many people like to think of themselves as overachievers. If you call yourself an overachiever, you're declaring that your standard practice is to go above and beyond what's necessary for achievement.

To be an overachiever, you must wholly embrace One More Try.

There is another critical component to this. Even though you may be willing to do the things that other people aren't willing to do, you must **be intentional and look for opportunities in everything you do**. That mindset must become second nature to you. When you practice this strategy long enough, it becomes a reflex. You don't think about it. You just do it.

On an even more fundamental level, you must believe that you can create a One More Try life for yourself. This is like confidence, but it's more about **creating a higher level of self-esteem**. Many people don't buy into themselves enough, and the limitations they live with come from within. Being your own worst enemy is something I've seen a lot.

I don't buy into this limiting mentality and I don't want you to either. It doesn't have to be that way!

I learned a long time ago that **we all have the wisdom inside us to create the future we want for ourselves**. Most of us simply don't tap into this rich vein, for whatever reason. We block that part of our identity and accept something less.

Sometimes we accept a lesser life because we weren't given a good role model to follow, or we've suffered through adversity that's made us mentally fragile. We wither under criticism and refuse to dig deeper to find the mental toughness and grit that even we didn't know we had.

Here's something that should excite you. When you do break through, the places where One More Try takes place are a lot less crowded than when you run with the pack. **Most people give up. They don't do the work you're willing to do. So, they won't get the results you'll get.**

Rather, when you move to this new place where One More Try is the norm, the law of averages is now working in your favor. Simply stated, more tries equal more successes.

That's a good place to start if you're looking for the boost you need to start implementing One More Try.

Busting Open the Piñata

One More Try is so important that I want to give you a few examples to drive home the point that often in life, it feels like we're making no apparent progress, even though we are.

My favorite of these is what I call "busting open the piñata."

Life is like taking swings at a piñata. It's also an excellent metaphor for how to understand the impact of One More Try. There's no external evidence that we're making progress and that's why people often quit before getting to the part of their lives where the candy comes out.

The perfect example of this is from a few years ago when I went to a birthday party for a 5-year-old. At the party, there was a piñata, and one by one, the kids put on a blindfold. They stepped up, were given a bat, spun around, and then told to swing at the piñata.

The first couple of kids grazed the piñata. They were disoriented and didn't know which direction to swing. Even with some well-intentioned help from their fellow partygoers, they did no apparent damage to the piñata. Or so it seemed!

Those kids got a little frustrated when nothing came out. What they didn't realize is that inside, the piñata was slowly breaking down.

The kids who went up later figured out the game a bit more. They stepped up, bat in hand, and took their swings. Many of them made solid contact and did some damage, whether they knew it or not.

The compounding effect of pounding on that piñata, even if it seemed like the piñata was holding firm, was making a difference. Every time a blow landed, those kids made invisible progress, growing ever closer to the ultimate goal of busting it wide open. All the kids shrieked with anticipation after each thump. After a few more whacks, they sensed the paper-mache beast was weakening. Still, the piñata would not break.

When all of the children had taken their swings, mom blindfolded the birthday boy and he stepped up for his turn.

That little man reared back, and with the mightiest "One More Try" you're ever going to see, he busted that piñata wide open.

You know what came next. More than a dozen children scurried to gobble up all the treats and goodies that had fallen from the piñata.

Was it that one shot that busted the pinata wide open? Absolutely not. It was the compounded accumulation of all those hits that contributed to achieving the goal of getting the candy.

Too many people quit their business, their workouts, or their relationships before the candy comes out! Although they're making progress, it doesn't always show up externally.

My advice to you is to keep hitting the piñatas of your life. Whether you can see it or not, you're making more progress than you might think.

Is this starting to sound like your life yet? It should. We all swing at a lot of piñatas and early on, we don't generally bust those piñatas open.

I told you at the beginning of this book that you were a lot closer to realizing your goals and dreams that you may think, and this is a perfect metaphor of that concept.

Just like the children, you're making **invisible progress** in your life. Unfortunately, most people don't stick around long to realize the outcomes from that progress.

However, when you know that you're moving forward, even when you can't directly see you're moving forward, you'll stay more focused on your processes and tasks to accomplish your goals.

Invisible progress is more than having faith. It's knowledge you've acquired because your efforts produced results on other things you've attempted in the past.

When we do bust open a piñata, we get an undeniable rush.

You've experienced it many times. You know exactly what that rush is.

In fact, the harder it is to bust open that piñata, the more intense the rush is. As we keep swinging, anticipation builds.

Adrenaline kicks in. Confidence grows. You may even get a little angry as you dig deeper and refuse to yield.

In your piñatas, the "candy" that tumbles out can be your bliss. It's your financial freedom. It's falling in love with the special someone in your life. It's landing the dream job you've always wanted.

All because you didn't give up. You gave it One More Try. And over time, those efforts compounded until you got precisely what you wanted.

You must tune out the naysayers and all the negative distractions to focus on busting your piñata wide open. You'll feel disoriented at times, doubt may creep into your mind, and you may think that your goal is not worth it. Until you learn how to win those battles, you'll never enjoy what your piñata holds for you.

If you stay with it long enough, you will enjoy the fruits of your labors. And everyone else in your circle who sticks around and supports you will enjoy those things as well.

Take your swings. As many as you need. Get that candy. There are a lot of piñatas waiting for you to bust open and enjoy.

A Father, a Daughter, and the Power of One More Try

I want to tell you what happened on April 26, 1998, and why that date means everything to me.

I was relatively new to the business world, and I was scheduled to give a presentation that night to 40 people on my team. The RSVPs didn't materialize the way I had wanted, and by the time the presentation rolled around, only eight people showed up.

I was crushed.

I started to doubt whether this was a career for me. I began to think maybe there was something better out there, something else that I was meant to do with my life. I was frustrated and discouraged and didn't know if I should keep doing this or not.

I sat down and had a talk with myself. It's as honest as I've ever been. Had I done everything I could for as long as I could? Had I done the right things at the right time? I really needed to decide if I had put forth my best effort to make a go of it.

Because I was candid with myself, the answer was "no." That's a hard thing for a proud man to admit to himself. Hard but necessary.

Even more important, I had to acknowledge my shortcomings. Until that point, I had followed a pattern of quitting when things got hard or embarrassing. I found it easy to pull the plug. Too easy.

Instead of walking away, I dug my heels in and decided I was going to give this one more try. I was going to empty my tank and do everything that I could to make sure that I had given my very best to my chosen profession.

Retreating and giving up were no longer options for me. I set my old limiting identity aside and launched a new version of myself. That "come to Jesus" talk with myself, that refusal to give in, and my decision to go the distance by tapping into One More Try changed my life forever.

From that night forward, my efforts and my mindset turned into a business life that has paid me hundreds of millions of dollars.

There's one more example I want to share with you.

Fair warning: there's a proud parent moment ahead. Those of you who are moms and dads will completely understand where I'm coming from.

As I write this, my daughter Bella is 17. Wow, where did that time go?

Much to her credit, she recently decided it was time to go out and get a job. Bella applied at a local pizzeria in town and had a great interview. They were ready to offer her the job until one final question tripped her up.

They asked if she was 18 yet. Since the pizzeria served beer, it was a minimum age requirement, and she didn't meet it.

Bella called me right after she left that interview. She was dejected when she shared the news. I was bummed. As a parent, when your child hurts, you do too.

But that's not the end of the story.

A half-hour later, Bella called again. The first words out of her mouth were . . .

"Dad, I got a job!"

Talk about somebody else getting candy from the piñata your daughter busted open. I can't even begin to tell you how elated I was. And, I was curious.

After a disappointing setback, most teenagers will tuck their tails between their legs and head home. But as she was leaving the pizzeria, Bella noticed a small café next door. Instead of passing by like 999 out of 1,000 job-hunting teenagers might do, she went inside and started talking to the hostess.

One thing led to another, and it turned out the café was looking to hire someone. And, that person didn't need to be 18! Bella met with the manager and was hired on the spot.

That's how my beautiful daughter, using One More Try, took a potential defeat and turned it into a victory instead.

I'm hard-pressed to come up with a more perfect example of how pushing yourself and using One More Try can work in your favor. It would have been so easy to give up, but because Bella made an effort to talk to one more business, she got a job, and it changed her life.

Perhaps the coolest part is that she did it all on her own.

Like father, like daughter.

It's one of the best proud parent moments I've had in my life.

Three Ways That One More Try Can Turn You into an Overachiever

Your path to becoming an overachiever is linked directly to One More Try. The more you try, the more you achieve.

Here are three overachiever principles to consider.

Extremity Expands Capacity

Your most significant gains don't come from places you're already at or where you've already been. **Your greatest gains and successes happen when you push yourself to new places and new limits.** You create an extreme condition compared to what you're used to, and when you do that, you expand your capacity for success. Your new level of capacity becomes your new norm.

As you become more comfortable pushing yourself to extremes, you become more confident because you know what waits for you on the other side.

If you're worried about pushing yourself to the point of exhaustion, don't be. I'm not saying that you shouldn't get your rest, but **I've found that most people are tired from too little activity, instead of too much activity**.

High degrees of activity produce energy, and you feed off this energy. Much like batteries, if you don't use your energy, you tend to lose it over time.

But when you use your energy, that produces even more energy. When you produce more energy, you can go to a more extreme place. Once you've been to that place, you're able to see it, feel it, touch it, and understand what that new level of capacity is to you.

Those of you who know me now know why I've adopted the motto MAXOUT. For 30 years, I've understood that **maxing out your life creates a new extreme level. That new extreme level creates a new capacity and the place where you will grow and achieve the most results.** In other words, when you MAXOUT, you will also MAXUP.

Winning Is a Numbers Game

If you want to be an overachiever, you must create better numbers for whatever is important to you.

Much of your success will come down to your commitment to executing basic tasks again and again. **You must learn to do simple things well.** You must be obsessed with perfecting processes repetitively until you create big enough numbers to give you the wins you're looking for.

Overachievers don't think in terms of quality or quantity. **They think in terms of quality *and* quantity.**

Tiger Woods doesn't just go through the motions when he practices hitting golf balls from two to four hours a day. He is obsessed with repetitively hitting each ball the right way with the same backswing, same stroke, and same follow-through each time.

If you watched *The Last Dance*, a documentary about Michael Jordan and the Chicago Bulls, you saw how hard Jordan pushed himself. You either got on board with Michael's level of practice and play, or you didn't last very long. Jordan didn't land in the record books by accident. He understood that you must put in the work and rack up the numbers when you practice, so that you can rack up victories of all kinds when you play.

The highest achievers always condition themselves to incorporate One More Try into their daily routines. As I mentioned, there's less competition when you rise to that level, and your victories will be bigger and better in all cases.

Perhaps you've coasted from time to time in your business. Maybe you haven't applied One More Try to its fullest advantage. Everybody goes through peaks and valleys, but you shouldn't wallow in those valleys for very long. You'll know when you're not putting forth your maximum effort. You'll know when you're not doing everything you can to make you and your business as successful as possible.

You can hide from yourself sometimes, but you can't hide from the numbers.

The numbers are a black-and-white reflection directly related to your effort. It's easy to compare month-to-month or year-to-year sales volume, phone calls, and other metrics. You should have no trouble keeping track of how often you go to the gym, how many sets and repetitions of weights you lift, or how many miles a week you go for a run.

You can't dominate when you don't crank out better numbers than your competitors or when measured against your past performance levels.

Nothing Creates Everything

In the beginning, God created the heavens and the earth. Now the earth was formless and empty, darkness was over the surface of the deep, and the Spirit of God was hovering over the waters. And God said, "Let there be light," and there was light.

—Genesis 1:1–3

Some theologians interpret Genesis as God creating the whole universe out of nothing. He just spoke existence into being out of total nothingness. I happen to be one of those people who also believes this, and I go into greater detail about my faith as part of One More Prayer in Chapter 18. This belief is known as *creatio ex nihilo* and is the answer to how the universe came to exist. *Creatio ex nihilo* teaches matter is not eternal but had to be created by some divine creative act, frequently attributed to God.

Here's how that applies to your life. **When you push yourself and empty everything you have inside of you to the point of having nothing left, that's when everything will be created.**

When you empty yourself, you create room for new experiences, goals, and efforts. Bruce Lee echoed that sentiment when he said, *"Empty your cup, so that it may be filled."*

I'm not talking about driving yourself to physical exhaustion. You should never put yourself in that state. What I am talking about is always doing One More. When you do, you're emptying yourself out. When you have nothing more to give, you have reached a state of *ex nihilo*.

And you're ready to fill yourself up in a higher capacity.

Making the Power of One More Try Work for You

Life won't hand you opportunities.

You need to be the type of person who goes out and creates opportunities for yourself. Don't wait! Be aggressive and understand that One More Try does not have to be perfect. It simply needs to be attempted. **When you hide from One More Try, all you're doing is disguising your insecurities.**

Even when you don't get exactly what you want, when you attempt One More Try, the next time you try again, you're not starting from scratch. You're going to be starting from a new level of experience that you can leverage to increase the odds of a better outcome.

As you implement One More Try, you'll also create new levels of capacity. These levels are where you'll find your most satisfaction. The more often you attempt One More Try, the more often you'll win because winning is frequently a numbers game, if you execute well and give your maximum effort. Also, keep in mind that you'll create new possibilities to fill up your life when you make every possible attempt and empty your tank.

The key to One More Try is to be **intentional**. You must have the strength and the focus to take steps that will drive you closer to where you want to be in life.

This is not always an easy thing to do. It requires a **quiet determination** to stay the course.

Or, as Mary Anne Radmacher once said, "*Courage doesn't always roar. Sometimes courage is a quiet voice at the end of the day saying, 'I will try again tomorrow.'*"

4

~~~~

One More and
the Five Principles
of Time Management

Every day is a new life to a wise man.

—Dale Carnegie

EVERYONE ACCEPTS THERE ARE 60 SECONDS IN A MINUTE. Sixty minutes in an hour. And most of us still think there are 24 hours in a single day.

You're probably thinking, "Of course, we do. That's how many hours there are in a day. Right?"

Not if you're high performer. Not if you're a One More thinker. Instead, what if I could show you how to bend and manipulate time to your maximum advantage? One More thinkers don't get 24 hours in one day.

I'm going to show you how we get three days in a single 24-hour block of time. I know it sounds crazy. But it's not.

As much as anything else, this principle has contributed to my success since I first started using it more than 20 years ago. Along with the other time management principles I employ, I've used it to triple the number of days I have, and that has helped me triple my amount of productivity.

One More thinkers perceive time differently. And now, I'm going to teach you how to do the same thing.

Your Relationship with the Perception of Time

Time is a constant. But we treat time as a variable. How often have you heard these expressions?

"Ugh! This day is taking forever".

"That month flew by".

And my personal favorite . . .

"I can't believe the weekend is over already".

Through our experiences, age, current circumstances, how much rest we get, and how busy we are, our perception of time is continuously shifting. **Scientists call this mind time, and it's completely different than clock time.** Mind time is what the speed of time feels like, and clock time is a constant chronology measured by the ticking hands of a timepiece on the wall.

Time is a fundamental element of our being and how we perceive the world around us. Our sense of who we are is shaped by how our brain connects our memories, present sensations, and our anticipation of the future. Neuroscientists, linguistic, psychological, and cognitive experts have studied the perception of time extensively for hundreds of years. Among other things, researchers know that **perceived duration is unique to every individual and does not focus on a singular sensory system**. Instead, time perception is a blended distribution system that involves the cerebral cortex, the cerebellum, and the basal ganglia.

Here's the takeaway. **Once you understand that you can alter how you perceive time, you can begin to bend time and use it to your advantage.**

Time Is Your Most Valuable Asset

Time is more valuable than money. Money is a replenishable resource. You can always add more dollars to your bank account, but you can't add more time to your life. **Your time is finite.** If you're 40, you can't turn back the calendar and become 30 again.

Authors, artists, songwriters, and poets have romanticized time throughout the ages.

The two most powerful warriors are patience and time.

—Leo Tolstoy, War and Peace

The wisest are the most annoyed at the loss of time.

—Dante Alighieri

My favorite thought about time may be the simplest and is attributed to Benjamin Franklin who said, *"Time is money."*

When your time is over, you get no replays. You can't reclaim time. However, our most valuable asset is frequently manipulated.

Mind time is perceived time and is directly related to the brain's interpretation of several variables.

As we get older, the rate that our brain processes mental images and how quickly they are perceived decreases. It's part of the natural aging process. Our vision and brain plasticity lessen, our neural pathways that transmit information degrade, and these shifts lead us to a sense of time speeding up. Even though an individual act happens in a fraction of a second, it takes longer to get to the same place. We lose that fraction of a second thousands of times a day.

There are several other variables we can't control as well. When we're physically tired, our brains can't transfer and process information as quickly. Our tired brains can't optimally see and make sense of visual, auditory, or tactile input. **Our reaction times slow, and this also makes us feel as if time is speeding up. In reality, it's just us slowing down in relation to the rest of the world.**

That's why athletes who aren't well rested will play a bad game. Their ability to process is thrown off. That knocks their sense of timing out of balance. They can't see or respond to in-game variables effectively, which is one of the reasons why even the best shooters in the NBA sometimes go 4-for-20 from the field.

Psychological trauma, drug use, intense feelings of fear or shock, ADHD, autism, depression, schizophrenia, and other factors also contribute heavily to altering perceptions of time.

The Five Principles of Time Management

Over the past 20 years, I've immersed myself in the concept of maximizing my time to accomplish my goals. What I discovered early on is that **you must respect the nature of time**. High achievers universally embrace this as a foundation of their success, including me.

As much as any other variable, **your relationship to time can profoundly affect how far you go in life**. I've tried all sorts of time management strategies. I've added and subtracted parts of various philosophies that make sense to me. And, eventually, I developed my own system that I refer to as the Five Principles of Time Management. If you can adapt and master these principles in your own life, you'll enjoy more success, make more money, be more productive, add layers of bliss, and build the life you were meant to enjoy.

Let's take a look at those five principles.

1. Add More "Days" to Your Day

One More thinkers should set aside the notion of a 24-hour day. The 24-hour day worked well before we had the internet, smartphones, wireless technology, computerized cars, jets, satellites, and other tools that let us expand our footprint and move at the speed of light.

We can now send an email anywhere in the world in an instant. We can hold a teleconference with dozens or hundreds of people 24/7. Instead of going to the library or digging through an encyclopedia, we can Google anything and get answers in a matter of seconds.

The ability to accomplish tasks has multiplied exponentially. Accessing information, people, and locations takes place with lightning-speed immediacy. That's why, if you want to be a high achiever, **the 24-hour day is an antiquated concept**. In my world, and for all One More thinkers, it no longer applies.

We're now able to accomplish more in five minutes, one hour, or one day than we could in an entire week or month 100 years ago. **Our ability to compress time *is* our ability to bend and manipulate time for our best purposes.** Guess what that does for your goals? It puts them in your face like never before. And when you're closer to a goal, you naturally approach it with greater urgency.

Here's a mindset you can put into practice today. It's effective. I've been doing it for more than 20 years now, so I know it works.

From time to time, you'll have one of those days where everything is falling in line. You're able to knock out a ton of stuff and be more productive in four or five hours than you are in one of your normal full days. Or maybe you've had a day where you knock out more than you have in an entire month. **What if you could replicate that rush every day?**

Here's how.

Instead of approaching your day as a single block of time, **divide your waking hours into three equal parts, or mini-days.** For me, that means my "first day" runs from 6 a.m. to noon. My "second day" is from noon to 6 p.m. And my "third day" is from 6 p.m. until midnight. **While you're living seven days in one week, I'm living 21 days in one week.**

To turbocharge how I spend my time, this is how I do it. By creating shorter days, my mind believes that each minute becomes more valuable. I don't waste time because **my sense of urgency is operating at a higher level**. Instead, I'm focused even more on what I need to accomplish "today." I compress work, relationships, productivity, fitness, and fun into shorter and more intense pieces of time with this strategy. **I shrink the finish line so that more of what I do becomes a sprint.**

Don't lose sight of the fact that your life is still in balance. You still make time for all parts of your life. All that you're doing is **squeezing useless air out of the wasted parts of your day**. At first, you may be intimidated by attempting to do this. But as you give it a try, you'll replace old bad habits with effective new ones. You'll move faster and have greater control of your time.

Here's the cool part if you implement this mindset. Imagine the compounding effect of working 21 days a week for a month, a year, or a decade. Or for the rest of your life. Now compare that to people you compete against who look at their days as a single 24-hour block of time. In my mind, I'm living more than 1,000 days in the same timeframe as others who think of themselves as living in a 365-day year.

Who has the advantage? You already know the answer.

I am a living example of what this strategy can do for you, and my results have been pretty good so far.

2. Approach Time with a Greater Sense of Urgency

The German philosopher Arthur Schopenhauer once said, "*The common man is not concerned about the passage of time, the man of talent is driven by it.*" Do you want to be common, or do you want to be a person of talent?

Urgency is the key. From my experience, there is a direct correlation between how fast you'll run versus how close you are to the finish line.

If you watch distance runners in a race, why does the last lap or leg of the race invariably produce some of the race's fastest times? In a 26-mile marathon, you keep a steady pace. As you get closer to the finish line, your adrenaline kicks in, and you find another gear. You push yourself because you're closer to completing your task and crossing that finish line. That produces a release of endorphins, and you feel that warm and positive rush.

Now think about running a 100-meter race. It's a flat-out sprint from start to finish. You approach the race with maximum urgency. A different mindset is required to do your best. Your body and your brain respond to a different set of stimuli.

It's not that people approach life with a lack of vision that causes them to fail. It's the type of vision they call on to get them across the finish line.

Your depth perception affects your ability to summon that sense of urgency required to perform better. When the goal is further away, you jog toward that goal. When it's right in front of you, it's a sprint.

Here's another example. You're a student who is assigned a major project at the beginning of the semester with a deadline toward the end of the semester. Do you jump on that project immediately? Most put that project on cruise control. They quietly slip it onto the top shelf of their life, knowing that they'll deal with it later. That is until the deadline starts to creep up.

At some point, panic, fear, dread, thoughts of "I hate college," and "I think I'll just become a bartender", kick in. But if you had attacked that project with a sense of urgency as soon as possible, the looming shadow, the boogieman, the beast you're facing, would be reduced to almost nothing.

If you apply this thinking to everything you do throughout the day, week, or year, you'll get more done and enjoy a sense of accomplishment that others only dream about.

3. Learn How to Control Time Instead of Time Controlling You

When you manage your time with a sense of urgency, you become the master instead of the servant. Moving faster puts you in control of your time more often than not. You have a sense of urgency, but you also have a greater say in what you think is important. That lets you spend more time on what's meaningful and rewarding to you.

Controlling your time is a mindset that should turn on as soon as your brain wakes up in the morning. If your mind is in the right place, controlling your time will start even before your feet hit the floor in the morning. As you're waking up, your brain is already planning your day. **Do you pay attention to what those first thoughts of the day are? The first 30 minutes of your day are critical.**

Think about the "timely" words of British statesman Lord Chesterfield: *"Take care of the minutes, and the hours will take care of themselves."*

How you approach the first 30 minutes of your day will set the tone for the balance of the hours to follow. That means staying away from your phone, computer, television, or any other forms of input that can distract you from what's important in your life. Instead, use that 30 minutes to plan out your day; review your meetings, phone calls, and projects; create priorities, meditate, pray, stretch, practice equanimity, reaffirm your standards, and update yourself on your goals.

Before your brain becomes cluttered with people, events, and information of the day, it has a chance to focus. Your brain receives the message that you're in control instead of the world controlling you. You're better able to start the day filled with confidence and the purposes that you choose.

Of course, surprises, changes, and redirection will spring up throughout the day. You react accordingly. But when you're not dealing with the unexpected, you're in greater control and working toward your life goals instead of reacting to everyone else.

In other words, **dictate the terms of your day, or your day will dictate those terms for you.**

4. Measure Your Performance Often

Where performance is measured, performance improves. Close proximity to measurement is critical. Every leading motivational and organization expert from Zig Ziglar to Peter Drucker builds this idea into their foundational strategies for a simple reason.

Measuring performance works.

As you shrink your timeframes and increase your urgency, you also need to shrink the intervals of how often you measure your performance. If you don't take time to measure, you'll have a more difficult time course-correcting. That leads to inefficiency and wasted time.

Just make sure you're measuring the right things. Be clear on your goals, priorities, and standards. Understand how they work in concert with each other. Learn to identify not only weaknesses but the potential sources of those weaknesses.

Legendary UCLA basketball coach John Wooden put it into perspective, saying, *"If you don't have the time to do it right, when will you have the time to do it again?"* Wooden was a stickler for doing things the right way, right down to how his players tied their shoes. He fine-tuned every technique and process on his teams for years, accepting only one standard and measuring the interim steps almost daily.

If your goal is to run a five-minute mile or to bump up your sales by 50 percent or your income by $50,000, how will you know if you're reaching these goals unless you look at the numbers? Anything less, and you're just throwing darts and hoping you'll hit your targets.

Average people assess themselves once or twice a year. But only making New Year's resolutions is not appropriate for One More thinkers. Top performers measure themselves monthly or weekly.

Do you take stock of your week's accomplishments on a Friday evening? Do you take stock and set your plans for the coming week on a Sunday evening? The top performers, the One More thinkers, go through this process daily.

There's even one more level beyond daily measurements. Some people measure themselves hourly. The most elite have an internal mechanism that is triggered with urgency. I have trained myself to do this, and I'm not lying when I tell you, as hard as it sounds, this discipline has served me well.

Think for a moment. Who's going to do better? The person who shrinks their measurement interval or the person who rarely measures where they're at? You already know this answer, too.

5. Focus on the Future

Too many people are stuck in the past. That kills their ability to be productive in the present. And robs them of making plans for the future.

The past is gone forever, but until you let go of it, the past is a thief and steals your ability to dream and imagine. You need to spend time thinking about your future because that's where you're heading. You must also stay connected to the present because that's how you build a better future.

It drives me nuts when I see so many people stuck in a loop of how their lives would be different today, "if only" that one big thing had been different. **People getting out of bad relationships or trying to distance themselves from poor family dynamics are particularly vulnerable to past thinking.**

This isn't to say you shouldn't address the trauma of your past. You must find a way to process it and move forward. If you can't, the only person you're hurting is you and the people you care about right now.

Conversely, don't fall into the trap of falling in love with your past if you've had great things happen, whether you earned an advanced college degree, got a big job promotion, got married, and so on. Those things are nice, but if you rest on those laurels too much, you're still not living in the present and building a better future. As Coco Chanel once said, *"Don't spend time beating on a wall, hoping to transform it into a door."*

One More thinkers have the innate ability to spend time dreaming and imagining about their future while taking decisive actions in the present to shape what lies ahead.

Changing Others' Perception of You

When you incorporate the Five Principles of Time Management into your life, how others see you is going to change, too. **When people see you're no longer wasting time, they begin to not waste your time.** They see you're also no longer spending too much time taking care of other people's priorities because you're too focused on taking care of your own.

At work, you need to be reasonable about this. Find a way to make your employer's goals your goals and blend the two to create harmony.

Your friends, family, and co-workers will understand that you're in an attack mode in your life instead of a react mode. They will respect you, and your relationships with them will be redefined. It's an added benefit that alters your life because your newfound time management is actually newfound life management.

Also, as you change your approach to time, you'll be open to meeting new like-minded people and embark on new projects and adventures you may have thought were just a pipe dream.

Let me leave you with this one final thought about time from Charles Darwin. *"A man who dares to waste one hour of time has not discovered the value of life."*

Stop wasting time and start bending time to your advantage to get on with the important things in your life.

5

One More Emotion

Unexpressed emotions will never die. They are buried alive and will come forth later in uglier ways.

—*Sigmund Freud*

LOVE AND HATE. JOY AND SORROW. PEACE AND ANGER. BLISS AND RAGE.

Why are emotions so important to understand? How do we use them to gain some measure of control in our lives? Because our lives are directly linked to the quality of our emotions.

Show me somebody who experiences bliss, joy, love, peace, and passion on a regular basis, and I'll show you someone leading an incredible life. Show me somebody who's dominated by hate, sorrow, depression, anger, and anxiety and I'll show you someone who is not leading a great life.

It's not the caliber of these people's homes, cars, or other material possessions that determines the quality of their lives. It's the quality of their emotions. **You have an emotional home that you live in. How you fill this home with the emotions you choose is the reality of your life, more than anything else.**

All of us experience five or six consistent emotions in this home every day. And no matter what your life conditions are, you will find a way to get those emotions. **Every one of us is conditioned to return to our emotional homes, even if those emotions don't serve us well.**

Have you ever noticed that no matter what's going on in your life, you always seem to find these same half-dozen emotions? For example, you may seek out worry, insecurity, fear, and anxiety, not necessarily because you want to. You do it because these emotions are familiar to you. **Your mind always seeks out what is familiar because there is a level of comfort, even when the familiar works against you.** The synapses in your brain are wired to seek and find those emotions.

You live in that emotional home. And the truth is, if you're going to change your life, you're going to have to clean house and change that emotional home.

This isn't to say that all emotions don't have their place in the world. What we perceive as an ongoing quest for positive emotions and avoiding negative emotions is a fallacy of sorts. **All emotions serve us one way or another.** Some anxiety is just as important as bliss or joy. Anxiety is a warning system our brain uses to protect us.

What we perceive as negative emotions serve important purposes in many cases, too. Think of emotions as neither negative or positive. Emotions just "are."

Both sides of your emotional quotient must be intentionally managed. **Too much of any emotion, perceived as either good or bad, doesn't serve you well.** Your goal should be to feel specific emotions in your emotional home, regardless of the external factors in your life, such as having a certain kind of job, living in a certain kind of house, or driving a certain kind of car.

The amazing thing is that when you have your emotional house in order, you're more likely to get that job, house, and car. So many people think that if they get those things, they'll feel the positive emotions associated with reaching those goals. One More thinkers flip-flop that sequence.

One More thinkers get intentional daily, weekly, monthly, and yearly with putting their emotional homes in order and deciding which emotions they most want to experience. **As a One More thinker, ask yourself, "What are the five or six emotions I most want to experience?"**

When you do this, the reticular activating system in your brain will go to work on finding the circumstances that will create those emotions for you. Once activated, harmful emotions will be decommissioned and replaced with positive emotions that will fully activate the best version of you.

Understanding the DNA of Emotions

The more you understand the genesis and relationship between all of your emotions, the easier it is to move away from destructive emotions and replace them with positive emotions.

Emotions are the primary driver of your personality. They heavily influence hundreds of decisions you make every day. Emotions are complex, sometimes unpredictable, and can

bubble up in ways and at times that you never expected. Plato said, *"Human behavior flows from three main sources: desire, emotion, and knowledge."* Desire and knowledge are what we acquire in response to stimuli we receive as we live our life.

Emotions are different. We're born as emotional creatures. Our emotions are constantly evolving, and the complexity of our emotional quotient is unique to each of us. They guide our actions and create part of the individual DNA of who we are.

Scientists know emotions are coded into our DNA as a "lower-level" response to outside stimuli. They are believed to have developed as a way for us to respond to different environmental threats, most notably the "fight or flight" response.

Emotions emanate from the subcortical areas of the brain, including the amygdala and the ventromedial prefrontal cortices. **When triggered, emotions produce biochemical reactions that have a direct impact on a person's physical state.** The amygdala also plays a role in releasing neurotransmitters, which are essential in creating memories. Without going too deep, this is why emotional memories are more robust and easier to recall.

All Emotions Have a Purpose

Like positive emotions, negative emotions are a valuable source of cognitive information to help you understand what's going on around you. They help you identify threats and to be on guard against possible dangers. **Negative emotions are an essential counterbalance to help you see both sides of a situation.**

While fear and anxiety are seen as negative emotions, they can be what spurs you to take action and change your life when you recognize their presence. If harnessed properly, negative emotions are motivators that help us address and correct behaviors.

Guilt is tied to our moral compass, and when we feel this emotion internally, we'll punish ourselves because we believe we've done something wrong. Guilt keeps us in check from doing bad things like committing crimes, cheating on our spouse or our taxes, or drinking and driving.

Similarly, jealousy is sometimes referred to as benign envy. This benign envy can motivate someone to believe that if another person can accomplish a goal, such as getting a good grade or hitting a high sales dollar amount, that it's tangibly in reach for them as well. **You can reframe jealousy as a good thing when you're able to view it as an achievable goal for you, too.**

The key is to keep these and other negative emotions in check. When we get caught up in an endless cycle of negative emotions, is when we get into trouble. Wallowing in negative emotions can impair our ability to think straight, especially when those emotions are incredibly intense.

You are your emotions. And if you don't get intentional about how you interact with your emotions and move toward the emotions you want, you'll live the same life you always have. **Once you learn to identify your emotions, they begin to loosen their grip on you. Your awareness means you're gaining control.**

As a One More thinker, you can begin replacing dominant harmful emotions with helpful emotions when you gain control. New and positive emotions will energize you. They'll help you chart new goals and directions. You'll find it easier to get big-ticket items done in your life when you live with confidence and happiness instead of doubt and despair.

Imagine what would happen if you could rebuild your emotional framework, one more emotion at a time, to put you in a position to become a millionaire, buy your dream house, or find your soul mate. Flipping your emotions from a "can't do" mindset to a "can do" mindset is an essential step to making all these things happen.

Why You Hoard Your Emotions

Changing your emotional mindset is a challenge, I'm not going to lie. There are mental barriers to overcome when you've been pre-conditioned to think a certain way, a way that brings you comfort and goes to great lengths to avoid pain. **Often, the actions you take in your life are because you think they'll give you a particular emotional response.** You buy flowers for your wife or girlfriend because you want to show your love for her and feel the love in return. You take a long walk on a beach or a hike alone in a park as a way to clear your mind and find peace. You work your butt off to reach a year-end work goal because you know you'll enjoy the recognition you receive and the pride you'll feel.

Emotions are stronger and more permanent than feelings. Feelings are emotional reactions. They're more transitory, and shallow in nature. Emotional responses run deeper and can be measured by physical cues. What mother's heart does not race when her child comes home from a long deployment in the military to surprise her? If you get in a fight with your spouse, at some point, they'll stop talking to you, but their body language will tell you all you need to know. Studies have even shown that unhealthy anger in its repressed state has been linked to cancer.

Unaccompanied by positive emotions, negative emotions can create an endless stream of ruminations. This repeated negative thinking increases the brain's stress levels, flooding our bodies with the stress hormone cortisol. That can lead to depression, overeating, drug and alcohol abuse, high blood pressure, and cardiovascular disease.

Although you want to hoard and experience only positive emotions, the fact is that all emotions are entirely normal to experience. That means anger, fear, disgust, sadness, contempt, shame, guilt, and other emotions we perceive as negative are just as normal as surprise, happiness, satisfaction, joy, and relief, to name a few. **When you try to repress perceived negative emotions in favor of only seeking and allowing positive emotions to exist in your mind, you tip a delicate balance that causes problems instead.**

Hoarding emotions dulls your ability to distinguish between reality and what you perceive to be reality. In turn, it creates an emotional clutter that can impact every part of your life. You've met people in your life who are off-the-scale deliriously happy, and you've met people who are in permanent downer mode. Both can be hard to be around. That's because both are shielding themselves from their genuine emotions by hiding in the midst of this emotional clutter.

The Act of Emotional Decluttering

Sorting through emotions in a way that helps you is an intentional process. Keep in mind that your actions may bring you certain material things and outcomes, but just as often, **you want the emotion attached to those outcomes.**

People are intentional about their actions, but rarely do we spend enough time thinking about the emotions attached to those actions. For this to happen, we must take a closer look at what we want. And we must be truthful when we do so. *Rich Dad, Poor Dad* author Robert Kiyosaki puts it this way: *"Emotions are what make us human. Make us real. The word emotion stands for energy in motion. Be truthful about your emotions and use your mind and emotions in your favor and not against yourself."*

People are a composite of a small handful of emotions they live with every day. These emotions create our emotional homes. Like any home, your emotional home may not be perfect, but it is comfortable.

Regardless of our physical environment, some of us do have a lot of positive emotions. In our emotional home, we routinely experience bliss, satisfaction, pride, and more. But others live in ugly homes dominated by resentment, anger, distrust, depression, and stress. These unwelcome visitors run amok and out of control.

And they damage us.

Much like all houseguests who stay too long, **we become desensitized to their hold on us.** They become our way of life. Making things worse, because we're programmed to go after things without paying attention to our emotions, when we fail, those bad feelings grow and grow.

The act of emotional decluttering means tossing out these unwelcome guests so that you can invite other more positive guests in for an extended, permanent stay.

Getting Honest and Intentional

One More thinkers must choose to change out harmful emotions. When you do, your emotional home will change. In fact, it's much like moving to an entirely new address.

It's not enough to take action to get the thing you want. We've all heard stories of people who have made fortunes but who also lead troubled and miserable lives. They live with fear, greed, and distrust, even though they might also live in a $10 million mansion and have $100 million in the bank.

They've fallen into the trap of believing they would be happy by default if they became wealthy. But the problem is, they didn't consciously choose to be happy. To practice gratitude. To be kind and generous. They were not intentional. And now, even if they outwardly appear to be one way, unless they've gotten past the overwhelming negative emotions, they're slowly dying on the inside.

Ask yourself, if you could choose to have $100 million in the bank, but you had no peace in your life, would you make that sacrifice? **What is the price of your joy and happiness?** Now, if you could choose to have $1 million in the bank instead but be completely content, surrounded by people you love and who love you back, and you looked forward to living every day, would you choose that instead?

As I said, changing out emotions is an intentional act and **an exercise in honesty**. As best-selling author Therese Benedict puts it, *"When you walk a life of honesty, you live a life of truth."* If you can't be truthful with yourself, what right do others have to expect that you'll be honest with them? Being honest and intentional are two of the best gifts you can give yourself. **Honesty is the springboard from which every** emotion emanates. **Intentionality is the muscle you need to get you to those honest emotions.**

Fortunately, if you set your standards and goals the right way, you can have both $100 million in the bank and be at peace with emotions that serve you well.

Filling Your Home with Positive Emotions

There are some actions you can take to move consciously toward reframing your emotional mindset. You'll have more success inviting the right kind of emotions into your house if you do the following:

- **Meditate.** When you slow your brain down, concentrate, and focus on what you want, your brain engages and moves you closer to those goals. When you consciously decide you want to release your anger or fear, you'll make room for peace and tranquility.

  I meditate daily to start my day. I clear out negative thoughts that don't serve me well. I practice gratitude and positivity. I focus on what I need to do for the day, and then I engage in my priorities. Above all else, I move forward, not backward.

- **Find balance.** If all you do is work, even though you may love it, you have no time for rest and recovery. Any setbacks or negative emotions can pile up and produce the oversized clutter I talked about. Dedicate time to activities and people that bring your life back into balance. For me, that might be a round of golf or taking my dogs for a walk. Both are relaxing breaks I need to restore my emotional health. Create new habits. Set new goals. Practice much-needed self-care routinely.

- **Identify your triggers.** This goes back to intentionality. Figure out what makes you angry or frustrates you. Can't stand it when people run late for appointments or cancel at the last minute? Is there a particularly annoying coworker who makes your skin crawl? Do politics, taxes, global warming, or child neglect light a fire under you? Take time to put your triggers into perspective. Some things you can change and control. And some things you can't. Manage your triggers, or they'll eat you alive.
- **Resolve to change the way you think.** Identify a negative emotion you'd like to rid yourself of or a positive emotion you'd like to enjoy more and make a conscious effort to move in that direction. As you do, consider what Proverbs 23:7 says. *"As a man thinks in his heart, so is he."*

When you're able to align your heart and your mind, you'll be ready to put the power of One More Emotion to work for you.

6

~~~

One More Association

You will never outperform your inner circle.

—*John Wooden*

WHEN YOU FINE-TUNE YOUR ASSOCIATIONS, you allow yourself to transform your actions and radically enhance your results. You could be one association away from changing your entire life.

As a One More thinker, you have an obligation to keep refining your peer group of friends and family members, so they add value to your thoughts, goals, standards, and outcomes. One of the most powerful dynamics in the world is to be productive and blissful in ways your peer group expects of you.

The bottom line is this: You may need to either change or expand who you associate with because **who you allow into your inner circle is critical**, and you must cultivate and invest in these people as a means of investing in yourself.

Your Relationships Define You

Your relationships directly impact how you function in the world. Since the day you were born, you've bonded with other humans. Your caregivers and immediate family were your entire world early on. As you grew, friends, others with shared interests, and your work associates became your focus.

You have been defined by all these relationships throughout your entire life. Some have added tremendous value. Others have been a big waste of time.

Consider the words of the poet John Donne, who wrote:

> *No man is an island,*
> *Entire of itself,*
> *Every man is a piece of the continent,*
> *A part of the main.*
> *If a clod be washed away by the sea,*
> *Europe is the less.*
> *As well as if a promontory were.*
> *As well as if a manor of thy friend's*
> *Or of thine own were:*
> *Any man's death diminishes me,*
> *Because I am involved in mankind,*
> *And therefore*
> *Never send to know for whom the bell tolls;*
> *It tolls for thee.*

Your associations bind you to the world. You're not an island. Instead, you're part of an interlocking web of humanity that shapes your identity based on your associations. It follows that **the people you spend the most time with are the people who will influence you the most.**

While you have some say over your relationships with your blood relatives, you can't change your DNA. You can choose to limit how you interact with family members who are toxic, overbearing, or naysayers. Unfortunately, familial relationships are complicated, so for the purposes of a One More thinker, **focus on relationships you have a lot more control over . . . your peer group.**

Your peer group is the most potent force and influencing agent in your world. You must place the utmost care as to who you let into this group. **To succeed in life, your peer group's standards must align with your own.** Their standards must become yours and vice versa.

William J. H. Boetcker said, "*A man is judged by the company he keeps, and a company is judged by the men it keeps, and the people of Democratic nations are judged by the type and caliber of officers they elect.*"

Be prudent in the company you keep. Like it or not, **you are the sum of your relationships, and you are judged for it**. Your relationships are a big part of how the world sees you. That can either work in your favor or against you.

If you're not getting all the results you want in life, take a look at your closest relationships. You may discover a relationship has grown stale, you have changed, the other person has changed, or time and distance mean the bond is no longer strong enough to benefit you.

When this happens, it's time for One More thinkers to consider the possibility of adding new and different associations to their lives.

Your Relationships Bull's Eye

Think of your relationships as a series of concentric circles, much like a bull's eye.

Each circular space represents different intimacy levels of the people you encounter in your life. The closer you get to the center of the circle, the closer you get to people who you connect with on a deeper and more profound level.

For example, the circle's outermost ring is filled with the strangers you meet daily. It could be the people sitting at the next table over in a sports bar, watching the same game as you. Or a business prospect who cold calls you to find out more regarding your goods or services. These strangers constantly make appearances in your life, and then they disappear, never to be seen or heard from again. In general, the impacts of strangers on your life are negligible.

Acquaintances are people you see from time to time, such as the butcher behind the meat counter at your grocery store or the parents of your son's or daughter's friends. Your small chats over time bind you to these people, and you enjoy random interactions when you bump into them.

Casual relationships draw you and others even closer. Think of these people as your outer circle of friends. They are your children's teachers, people you see at house parties, and members of the same clubs or organizations you belong to. You invest your relationship energy with them on a limited basis. You're comfortable sharing information, and you tend to like these people, but your relationship with them is guarded, and you don't go out of your way to have them in your life.

The innermost circle is small and consists of just a few people who impact you daily. These people could be your spouse, children, or parents. But that's not always the case. There are no hard and fast rules that say blood relatives are immediately granted access. **Not all life-long friends and family members end up being in your inner circle**, and that's okay. You can still be close to those people. Their relationships are valued and worthy of your time and commitment.

Your inner circle could have a mentor, or a business partner who has worked by your side to grow a shared enterprise from scratch into a success. It could be a friend you just "click" with. There's a bond of trust, commitment, and familiarity that brings you close, and no set timetable on how quickly these inner circle relationships develop. Some take years, and others can happen in a matter of months.

These bonds remain fluid, and when they do change, that's when you need to consider new associations.

You are at the center of all these circles. **You are *the* bull's eye.** The nature of life is that people enter your life, and they move closer to the center of the bull's eye, or they move away. It may take years or as quickly as a matter of weeks, but people rarely stagnate in one circle for your entire life.

That is another way of explaining the expression that people enter your life for "a reason, a season, or a lifetime." **Eventually,** each person's association with you is revealed. When that purpose has been realized, your relationship changes, and other new associations move in to fill the void.

The people in each of these circles influence your life. The closer they get to the center of the circle, the more potential for ongoing, meaningful dialog and impacts on you. The boundaries between these circles are fluid and dynamic. Relationships constantly change, and people will move from one ring in the circle to the next depending on how your life or theirs changes. Time and circumstances create this swirling flow of people moving from one circle to another all the time.

A Closer Look at Your Inner Circle of Friends

All the circles in your life influence you to some degree or another. But it's the associations you have with your inner circle that influence you the most. That's why, when you add or drop an association in your inner circle, you'll experience the most change.

Think about the small group of friends you're closest to in your life. Who are the two, three, or four people outside of your family who you've spent the most time with over the past 90 days? Do those people have two or three things in their life, whether it's material possessions, business success, fitness level, spirituality, or other emotions they experience, that you desperately want in your own life? If you can't quickly identify those things, these relationships may not serve your inner circle's needs.

People can still bring value to your relationship with them, but for the purposes of this discussion, I'm talking about associations that can change your life. If they don't have anything in their life that you don't have but want, it's time to re-evaluate whether you should seek other associations to meet your needs.

Conversely, if these people have things in their lives you desperately don't want, such as being broke, unfit, constantly angry, lazy, and so forth, then you need to evaluate your proximity to them immediately. Even if they love you and you love them back, you still need to assess your proximity to them because what they have will influence what you will get.

It's an ongoing process of adding people to your life who have the things you want the most. That's how it works. **Proximity to people causes familiarity, and our brains move toward this familiarity.**

Quality over quantity is essential as well. Even a small amount of time spent with the right couple of people can make a large difference. You lean on and learn from each other. You laugh and mourn with them and feel what they feel. They are genuinely happy for your successes, and you are just as delighted with theirs. There is a reflected glory when one of your closest friends succeeds because you feel like you're succeeding, too.

Think of some of the synergies growing out of famous inner circle friendships. Steve Jobs and Steve Wozniak. Tina Fey and Amy Poehler. Warren Buffett and Charlie Munger. Ice Cube, Dr. Dre, and NWA. Oprah Winfrey and Gayle King. The list is endless.

Great art or accomplishments of any kind are often a single person's vision but realized with the help of inner circle of friends who bring that passion to life.

Think about bands like the Foo Fighters, Imagine Dragons, Florida-Georgia Line, Green Day, Linkin Park, or any other group that's made it big in the music business. They're all excellent examples of a collaborative effort working toward a single vision.

When you and your inner circle are in alignment, all of your lives flow. Loads are lighter. Your confidence reigns. You are blissful. You radiate these positive things outward to all parts of your life and the lives of others.

Sometimes, though, your inner circle no longer adds the value you need. Through no fault of yours or theirs, life changes. It's amazing how fast someone can fall out of favor or become a stranger compared to the person you once knew.

As your life changes, your friends will change too. Their thoughts and beliefs will change. You will continue to grow, and they may not. It can be a tough time when you come to this realization. Deep down, you'll know. Then you'll have to decide how you want the friendship to change.

People ease in and out of our lives all the time. **Everything has an expiration date**, and the sooner you accept that a friendship, while still having value, does not meet the criteria required to meet your highest-level needs, you'll accept that you probably need to find a new association in your life. You must then intentionally choose to move these people from your inner circle to your outer circle, giving you the opportunity to maximize the potential for new inner circle associations.

Just like cars need regular maintenance, so too do your associations. Evaluate whether the proximity of the people in your inner circle is still appropriate or not. Don't be flippant about this. **Be honest about what you need out of the people**

you need the most. As Benjamin Franklin cautioned, "*Be careful when choosing a friend. Be more careful when changing a friend.*" Words that hold just as much meaning today as they did more than 200 years ago.

Don't take this responsibility lightly. But don't neglect it either, simply because you don't want to make a difficult choice. One More thinkers recognize that relationships expand and contract over time. This movement allows for One More association to add immeasurable value and give us more of the life we deserve.

Auditioning Your Inner Circle

Family dynamics can be challenging. For the most part, we accept that some of our immediate family members are part of our inner circle. You can't choose your family members, but you choose who else you can admit to your inner circle of friends. How you decide who these people are will impact a big part of your life, so deliberate carefully.

For me, anywhere from three to five friends works best. Your inner circle may be a bit smaller or larger. **But don't get hooked on the idea that you should have 15 or 20 people in your inner circle.** You dilute the quality of the associations you'll need to rely on at the highest level if you do. That's also a lot of people to keep up with, and you'll exhaust yourself in the process.

The people you allow into your inner circle are among the most important choices of your life. Choose wisely, and your life is propelled to new levels of bliss and productivity. Choose poorly, and you'll suffer the slings and arrows of a life poorly lived.

The question then becomes how do you properly evaluate the criteria for admission into your inner circle?

You will have certain biases based on your values, beliefs, and experiences that you'll employ. There is no magic formula. Some of your decisions are made by intuition. Some are based on your history with a person. Regardless, admission to your inner circle should come organically, over time.

There are some high-level qualities to consider as you make your decisions. The people in your inner circle should have a fully developed sense of emotional maturity. They need to be steadying influences who are happy and highly productive. They must be loyal and make rational decisions based on reason instead of impulse.

Reverse engineer the process of examining your associations. If you meet someone who knows what they expect for their own lives, then as a close associate, that's what you should expect in yours as a byproduct of your relationship.

Unhappy people are not emotionally mature and won't serve your relationship well. Whether it's a friend, co-worker, or family member, do your best to limit your interaction with them. You can still be cordial and maintain a relationship with these people. **But don't get sucked into their negative emotional vortex at your own expense.** You'll pay a significant price if you do.

If you see things that turn you off and they are not likely to change quickly or easily, then these are people you should keep at arm's length or eliminate from your life. Not easy. But, oh so necessary for One More thinkers.

Your inner circle must also consist of good human beings. They must treat others well and be free from fear, anger, and prejudices that could hurt others by their thoughts and deeds. They must be above ethical reproach, compassionate toward those less fortunate, and protective of children, the elderly, and those with limited mental or physical capacities.

Your inner circle should also inspire you at a visceral level. You should be able to feel that "buzz" when you're around these people. You look forward to the dopamine release you know is coming when you're with them.

Apply your standards for your inner circle as well. You want sharp business minds, entrepreneurs, or analytical types who can balance your shortcomings and help you achieve your goals. **Joining together, these associations make you greater than the sum of your parts.**

Think of several traits that immediately come to mind that your inner circle should have. Can your inner circle help make you whole in your financial affairs, your relationships, emotional health, faith, physical well-being, or provide the love every person needs? If these people can't elevate your essential needs in your life, they don't have qualities that serve you, based on what you need. This isn't to say you can't be friends, because of course you can. Don't jettison a person who doesn't fit the needs of your inner circle. Instead, keep looking to add someone who does.

Realigning people in the various circles in your life isn't easy. Distancing yourself from someone who is no longer compatible with your changing thoughts, beliefs, and goals can produce guilt that's hard to overcome. But sometimes, it's necessary. You can control only your thoughts and actions. You can't control others. **If people choose to think and do things that are counterproductive to you living your best life, then it's incumbent on you to make the choices that best serve you.**

When you linger in bad relationships, you don't make room for better relationships, those One More associations that change your life for the better and forever. Accept that some people will make the cut, and some won't. Be fair but firm as you reach these kinds of decisions.

Let me leave you with one final thought from Vincent Van Gogh about one of the greatest gifts your innermost associations can offer:

"Close friends are truly life's treasures. Sometimes they know us better than we know ourselves. With gentle honesty, they are there to guide and support us, to share our laughter and our tears. Their presence reminds us that we are never really alone."

7

<!-- decorative ornament -->

One More Dream

Let go of the past and go for the future.
Go confidently in the direction of your dreams.
Live the life you imagined.

—*Henry David Thoreau*

CHILDREN ARE DREAMERS. THEIR IMAGINATIONS ARE THE RULERS OF THEIR DREAMS. They're naturally curious. These things make children the happiest people on Earth. And great teachers, too.

Entering Your Dream State

The happiest people in life operate out of their imaginations and dreams, and not their histories.

Stop! Read that sentence again. This is one of the single most powerful takeaways for a One More thinker. To be happy, successful, and productive, operate out of your imagination, your dreams, and your vision.

Reframing your entire mindset is not a subtle action. It requires concentrated effort for an extended period to break pre-existing ingrained thought habits.

There is no way you will experience your best life if you try to operate out of your history or memories of your past. It can't be done. Pause for a moment and let that sink in a bit more.

A Child's Lesson for You

A 4-year-old, and children of all ages, are happier because they operate in the here and now. Their hearts and minds are filled with reverie, fantasy, and creativity. Their past doesn't weigh them down because they have no past.

At one time or another, most young boys and girls pretend they're Batman, Spiderman, a Disney princess, or Barbie as they go about their play. They are the blissful products of their unfettered minds. I believe children are also happier because being born recently means they were closer to God in a less distant past.

Think about the frequency of your dreams. When was the last time you had your Batman or princess moment? Do you intentionally visit your imagination often? I'll bet most of you don't. Even though one of the best parts about dreaming is how much it costs.

Dreaming is free.

More than that, **dreaming is one of the greatest gifts we can give ourselves. Yet, almost nobody takes advantage of it.** The sad part is that a lack of dreaming will cost you everything. When we don't dream, we rob ourselves of creating beautiful memories in the future. There's a sad irony to that. Instead, as we get older, many of us are weighed down by our pasts. We struggle against heavy memories that get in our way of living a blissful life.

How often do you dream?

And how often do you think about your career or how your boss has treated you over the years? In your personal life, have you obsessed about a rocky marriage? Have your parents, siblings, or friends hurt or betrayed you? Have you suffered through a string of health or financial setbacks?

Think of your past like suitcases filled with cement. As heavy as those bags are, many of us are afraid to put those bags down because carrying them around is all we know. Even though you don't like those bags, there's a sense of security because those bags are full of familiarity. That's why your brain likes going back there.

Over time, the cement in those bags multiplies, and your brain becomes heavier and more cluttered with life's challenges and adult worries.

We also use our imperfect past to create a flawed vision of the future. Then we go live that future. And we get stuck. We have a hard time getting out of our **mental quicksand**, which leaves us feeling like we're drowning. As adults, there is a direct connection to a lack of how happy and productive we are and our addiction to operating out of our memories. To live a better life, **we must consciously choose to operate out of our dream state and not our past.**

Why You're Trapped in Your Past

Although you're growing, learning more, and doing more, why aren't your emotions, productivity, and happiness changing? Because you're stuck in a thought pattern—**a replay loop continuously linked to your past.** The worst part is that these patterns are unconscious. You could go for years and not realize you're stuck in them.

I point out these patterns to you so you can break out of them by raising your awareness. **Patterns and loops lose their power over us once you become aware of them.** Awareness is kryptonite to negative thought patterns. Once you're aware, you can change an existing pattern by dreaming of a dramatic and compelling future. The past is the past.

Can you recognize negative patterns of emotions or actions in your current life? It shouldn't be too hard. A bad relationship? A dead-end job? A chronic substance abuse problem?

What if you could create child-like patterns rooted in dreams and imagination instead of dwelling on past negative thoughts? Old patterns create contentment in your brain. One of your brain's primary functions is to protect you from perceived threats as part of the "fight or flight" response. There is no need to take flight to something that's already taken place.

By our nature, we crave order. We are hard-wired to be problem-solvers because solving problems feels good. And that's also why we're intimidated by our unknown futures. We can't apply the same level of certainty in our lives to things that haven't happened yet. But the truth is you're only hurting yourself.

That isn't to say you should shut off your past. Many people find joy in continuing to connect with the same people, places, behaviors, and rituals that define their lives. Of course, there's a place for that in your life.

But if that's all you're doing, you're selling yourself short.

Moving into Your Future

The first step of moving from your past to your future is acceptance. Deepak Chopra teaches us, "*I use memories, but I will not allow memories to use me.*" **You know what gets swept aside when you hold on to your past? Your entire future.**

More than 60 years ago, President John F. Kennedy also understood the importance of looking to the future when he said, "*History is a relentless master. It has no present, only the past rushing into the future. To try to hold fast is to be swept aside.*" Those words still ring true today.

Think of moving into your future this way. Your brain, thoughts, and emotions are like a glass that can only hold so much liquid. In this case, that liquid is your past. When you fill a glass to the rim with your past, it's impossible to fill it with anything else until you empty that glass, no matter how hard you try. Making peace with your past is how you empty that glass and create room for your dreams and your future.

Just don't spend too much time trying to make peace with your past. When you do this, you use up valuable time better spent looking toward your future. Visualize pouring out your past thoughts. See the empty glass. Then be intentional by filling that glass with ideas that spring out of your imagination.

Embrace your future. Fill your glass with your vision and personal possibilities instead of drowning in stale thoughts that no longer serve you well. Do whatever it takes to set aside the past and set your sights on the future.

Another path to acceptance is acknowledging that the total of all you are today is the result of your past. Your pain, flaws, and barriers are counterbalanced by the strength, wisdom, and knowledge you've gained over the years. Embracing the total of all you already are gives you the tools to use as a springboard to your future.

Still not convinced?

It's not your future that you're afraid of. It's your past that makes you anxious and scared to dream.

Putting Your Imagination to Work

Thomas Edison had a beast of an imagination. The world would be a much different place today if Edison had lingered in his past instead of using his imagination to shape humanity's future.

He once said, *"To invent, you need a good imagination and a pile of junk."* Apparently, Edison kept a lot of junk around. It took him more than 1,000 attempts before he invented the first commercially viable light bulb.

Keep in mind, that was just one of Edison's inventions. He created the phonograph, the motion picture camera, the mimeograph, alkaline storage batteries, and even concrete and cement. In all, Edison was credited with 1,093 U.S. Patents in his lifetime. Worldwide, he's credited with 2,232 patents. Yes, those are records.

Edison was a pretty good businessman as well. He amassed $200 million of wealth in today's dollars during his lifetime. Do you think he got there being bound by the failures of his past experiments? Not a chance. Edison is also credited with saying, *"I have not failed. I've just found 10,000 ways that won't work."* The world would be a much darker place, literally, if he had failed.

Dreams are the product of your imagination at work. Imagining is therapy. It's healthy. So, one of the best ways to be good to yourself is to put your imagination to work.

Many people think of dreams as unconscious thoughts your brain manufactures when you're asleep. But the kinds of dreams I'm talking about are your lucid dreams.

You're more in control when you're awake, and while there's value in letting your subconscious work out your dreams and direct your energies when you're asleep, **I believe your best dreams take place when you're wide awake.**

What makes humans unique is that our consciousness allows us to extend beyond the confines of present time and space. This other dimension is our dream state, where imagination flourishes. That dimension is both wildly exciting and infuriatingly inexact. It's a place where you free yourself from your inhibitions, worries, and thoughts of the past. **Therapists have long called this reconnecting with your inner child.** Now you know why.

If you're a logical and orderly thinker, it's okay to search for your future vision instead of getting hung up on the label of "dreaming" too much. Dreams and visions are interchangeable.

No matter what you label it, **you'll be energized by your vision, imagination, and your dreams. And if you're lucky, you'll feel uncomfortable, too. Uncomfortable is good.** Uncomfortable is necessary progress. Uncomfortable means your imagination is working to plug in disparate thoughts to create something new. Remember, the past is familiar. The future is unknown.

Uncomfortable is one of the necessary emotions you need to move forward. So, **hold tight to those uncomfortable feelings.** They're valuable parts of the future you.

Giving Yourself Permission to Dream

Granting permission to live in your imagination and create dreams is one of the greatest gifts you can give yourself. There will be hurdles to overcome. You'll get stuck in self-editing thinking.

Would people laugh at me if I did this? Could I lose friends or damage my reputation if I dare to do what I'm imagining? Should I conform and just do what's expected, even though it will make me unhappy?

All of these are "fear" questions. And as I've noted, all of them are based on the shackles of your past.

One way to permit yourself to dream is to forgive others for past wrongs. More important, **you need to forgive yourself.**

Dr. Wayne Dyer was fond of saying, *"Forgiving others is essential for spiritual growth."* That spiritual growth releases you from a lot of useless anger and pain. **Spiritual growth is directly linked to dreaming and your imagination.** It's another part of that other dimension so vital to living your most blissful life. Spiritual growth is also another way you empty your glass to make room for new dreams.

Dreaming requires a bit of self-analysis too. You have deeply ingrained mental patterns and habits you're not aware of simply because you've carried around that dead weight baggage for so long:

I can't.
I won't.
That's not me.
I'm not good enough.
I'm too fat.
I'm too old.
I'm too young.

You get the idea. The list of mental boulders blocking your path is endless. All they do is make you sad, stressed, depressed, and filled with anxiety. Once you identify those negatives, you can reduce or eliminate them through a better quality of intentional thinking. **Replace negatives with dreams and visions that are exact, specific, and repetitive.**

Your dreams are best fueled by new ideas, thoughts, and thinking from unlikely sources. Quality dreams come from priming your mental pump with a wide variety of things that interest you. **Your brain, energized by your imagination, will** set about the work of linking these seemingly unrelated thoughts to create ideas that may leave you amazed.

Understand that our subconscious minds can't tell the difference between reality and an imagined thought. That's why the things we focus on and continually think about eventually manifest in our lives.

Just as imaginative thinking is not linear, so too is the timeline when your brain creates new dreams for your consciousness. Ever wake up in the middle of the night with the answer to a problem that's been vexing you for weeks? Have you been jolted with the solution to a thorny problem when you're at your kid's baseball game, while you're walking through Home Depot, or taking a morning shower?

Your imagination has no concept of night and day. No brain says it will dispense ideas and solutions during a staff meeting at 11 a.m. every morning. It comes when it comes. Pay attention when it does. **Then take steps to record or remember your thoughts. Your subconscious has worked hard on your behalf, and it would be downright rude to let those thoughts slip away.**

Dreaming and Doing

The Power of One More is about thinking *and* doing. Up until now, we've talked a lot about the thinking part of dreaming. It's just as critical to put your dreams into actions that will push you toward your goals.

In a baseball game, you can't be on both first and second bases simultaneously. Likewise, in life, you can't live in two places at one time. To steal second base, you must take your foot off first. Guided by your dreams, take your lead off first and make a break for the next destination in your life.

You can either choose to stay stuck and live in your past. Or you can choose to live your best life by dreaming and choosing to live in your future.

When you **intentionally act upon your dreams**, you'll be amazed at how you naturally attract what you need. You'll start to understand that along with bad habits, people who are bad for you will also fade into your past. As this happens, you'll begin to realize that **it wasn't always the relationship that you valued. It was how the relationship made you feel.**

New dreams rewire your life, and when you make room like an empty glass, you'll fill your life with new relationships and adventures. Along with your gut, intuition, and your imagination, your dreams will start to manifest in a way that lightens your load. You'll see exciting new possibilities as you move toward your future.

You will be a much happier person when you take your One More dreams and turn them into your new reality.

8

～✦～

One More Question to Ask Ourselves

The unexamined life isn't worth living.

—*Socrates*

DO YOU EVER THINK ABOUT WHAT YOU THINK ABOUT?

That is a really powerful question I ask. It's one of many questions I'm going to ask you in this chapter and a question you should be asking yourself.

The truth is most people never do. **Most people never take control of their thoughts because they don't ask the right**

questions, so they have a flawed belief of what their thinking should be. That leads to an equally fundamental question.

What is thinking?

Simply put, thinking is the process of asking and answering questions of yourself. That's how thought works. You constantly ask and answer questions in your head thousands of times a day.

So, if you want to change the quality of your thoughts, you need to change the quality of the questions you ask. It's the quality of the questions you ask that controls the quality of the thoughts you think. You'd be amazed at how finely tuned your brain is at finding you the answers you're looking for.

Does that make sense to you?

This could be a foundational seismic shift in your life if you begin to ask better questions. **Better questions lead to better answers. Better answers lead to a better life.** Most people don't do this. But One More thinkers do. Most people ask questions that make them weaker, less resilient, or less resourceful. They take the easy way out. In some cases, these questions do harm by creating fear, anger, distrust, or a lack of confidence.

The Navy Seals are taught to ask the question, "What in this situation can I control immediately?" By contrast, most people ask themselves, "What could go wrong? What can't I control in this situation? What should I fear and worry about?" because most of us are hard-wired to think that way.

If you ask those types of questions, you're always going to find yourself under duress. The answers to those questions are the answers your brain is going to find for you. Self-examination is a critical process to uncover wisdom in your life. **When you ask the right questions, you arrive at the truth about yourself.**

Unfortunately, looking inside your own life is not always fun. Your inner voice can be your most vocal critic, and self-accountability means there's no place to hide. But to achieve personal growth, One More thinkers must accept this challenge and embrace answers to the big questions in their lives.

Many times, people find it only takes one more answer to produce dramatic changes. **Asking the right questions is the first step to getting the answers you need to make that happen. Getting answers removes roadblocks that help you create change.** It's difficult to fix problems anywhere else in your world until you have your own house in order.

Eugene Ionesco said, *"It is not the answer that enlightens, but the question."* You humble yourself when you challenge yourself to be better. And the best way to do this is by questioning the foundation of your thoughts and actions from day to day. The answers to these big questions are as unique as you are. There are no right or wrong answers. There is no one-size-fits-all solution. In many cases, it's like peeling back the layers of an onion because the questions you ask will lead to new questions based on your experience, memories, feelings, and relationships.

Face these questions. Embrace the answers. If you're honest with yourself, you'll break through barriers that will lead you to an extraordinary life.

What if you could find One More powerful question to ask yourself several times a day? It's impossible for me to guess what questions and answers are important to you. Instead, I've put together the following list to start your self-examination process. Certain questions will resonate with you. Pay attention. That's your "inner you" trying to tell you something important.

Don't rush through these questions and the answers you uncover. Let the questions linger. Find a quiet place and let your mind go to work so the answers will have value for you. Also, think about the answers you come up with today versus the answers you'd like to have at some point in the future. Once you plant these future answers in your brain, your mind will go to work on your behalf to turn these answers into a new reality for you.

Remember, one answer can create big changes. And asking One More questions is the first step to that desired outcome.

One More Questions to Ask Yourself to Lead an Extraordinary Life

1. What one more thing can I do to show my spouse or my partner I love them?

2. How can I do one more thing to improve my relationship with my children?

3. Is there one more thing I can do to make my family feel more special?

4. Is there one more thing I can do to show my appreciation to the people I work with?

5. What's one more way I can adjust my thinking so I make fewer excuses?

6. What part of this situation can I control right now?

7. How is this happening for me and not to me?

8. What's one more thing I can do to calm myself down today?

9. Is there one more thing I can do to bring myself long-term peace?

10. What's one more way I can worry less about what other people think?

11. What's one more way I can bring my anger level down?

12. Is there one more thing I can do so people will see me less different than I see myself?

13. What's one more way I can worry less about the past?

14. How can I implement one more way to worry less about the future?

15. What's one more way I can get more excited about the future?

16. What's one more way I will practice gratitude?

17. How do I implement one more way to procrastinate less and protect the valuable asset of my time?

18. What's one more way I can be less of a spectator and more of a participant?

19. Can I do one more thing to ask myself hard questions even if I know I won't like the answers?

20. What's one more way I will tell myself it's okay to fail and learn from my mistakes?

21. Is there one more way to be a good steward with the money I have been blessed with?

22. What's one more way to ensure my values are consistent with my standards and goals?

23. In my work, is there one more way I can become an effective leader?

24. What one more way can I become healthier?

25. How can I make one more change to my diet to lose weight?

26. What's one more exercise I can do at the gym to burn fat or pack on muscle?

27. What's one more thing I can let go of that's been holding me back and that I'm better off without?

28. How do I give myself one more block of time to let my mind wander and daydream?

29. What's one more thing I can eliminate that's stopping me from doing the things I could be doing?

30. What's one more way I can change my thinking so I complain less?

31. Is there one more thing I can do to help somebody in pain who really needs me?

32. What's the one more thing that has provided me with the most bliss recently?

33. How can I do one more thing to handle conflict better?

34. What's one more thing I can do to better deal with the people in my life who drain the energy out of me?

35. Is there one more thing I can do to carve out more time to be mindful and intentional?

36. What's one more thing I should do to stop holding grudges?

37. What one more thing have I learned in life that I can pass on as a mentor to others?

38. What's one more thing I can do to enjoy my work more?

39. Was I curious enough to ask one more question to seek out answers to important questions in my life today?

40. What's one more prayer I need to have or scripture I need to hold closer in my faith life?

41. Is there one more way I can thank and honor my God for the gifts I received today?

What Are the Answers?

Answers to these questions may make you uncomfortable. Not always. But in many cases, to grow, **the best answers will be the most difficult for you to address**.

You've heard the saying that there are no dumb questions in life? Not true! There are dumb questions. They're the ones you ask that don't challenge you. They're the ones that provide you with convenient truths. You only cheat yourself and waste time when you ask yourself and others dumb questions. Making things even worse, deep down, you know when you're doing this.

If you want to be average . . . if you're happy where you're at because you're comfortable, scared, or lazy, and you don't want to know how to make your life better, then don't ask the questions that lead to your growth. Nobody can force you to do anything you don't want to do.

"The greatest gift is not being afraid to question," Ruby Dee once said. If you're not healthy enough to want to gift yourself with the truth, then don't get to the end of your life with regrets.

Some questions won't have immediate answers. Don't assume defeat if you can't apply logic and solutions when that happens.

An answer to a question you ask now may not come until later. Or not at all. Give yourself credit for having the courage to ask the question and seek the answer. Remember, one question often leads to another, and another, and another.

Enlightenment travels a lot of different paths. Learn to live with the great unanswered questions in your life. Seek the answers daily. Some will come to you like a lightning bolt. Others will come to you over time.

Either way, living with the extraordinary questions and answers of your life is one of the most admirable traits of a One More thinker.

9

One More Goal

*May He give you the desire of your heart
and make all your plans succeed.*

—*Psalm 20:4*

THROUGHOUT OUR LIVES, WE'VE BEEN
INUNDATED WITH SYSTEMS, PHILOSOPHIES,
AND METHODS ABOUT HOW TO SET GOALS to
make our life better. There's *definitely* no shortage of resources
on the subject.

It would be naïve for me to think you're not already using
some kind of strategy related to your goals. Instead, I want to
improve how you approach your goals and goal-setting process.

Here's a good place to start.

I believe goals are energy. Goals are a life force. Goals are a state of being. They're more than a manifestation of the ideas, hopes, desires, and dreams you have inside of you. The pursuit of your goals, when properly executed, is the **transference of energy into action**, creating one of the purest forms of One More in your life.

Too often, though, goals aren't designed as a conscious decision to improve your life. Often, you set goals as a reaction or a response to something that is happening in your life. Instead of playing defense, the key is to **proactively fill your mind** with the right kind of thoughts about your goals. When you do, your entire being is invigorated to accomplish those goals.

That's because the mind always gravitates to what it is familiar with and draws in whatever resources are necessary to propel you forward. **What you think leads to what you need.** When you consciously access what you need, your mind sets about the business of making your goals a reality.

The Relationship Between Standards and Goals

I go into standards in greater detail in Chapter 10, but I want to briefly make sure you understand why goals and standards are linked together and how they work in tandem for your benefit. Many confuse the two, but they aren't the same.

You create goals based on desired outcomes that start as thoughts in your mind. For example, "I'd like to make enough money to donate $10,000 to my favorite charity," or "I want to take a trip to Europe this summer," are worthy goals. But without a plan of attack to achieve those goals, they have a much less chance of becoming a reality.

Your first order of business is to **figure out what you're willing to tolerate** to meet your goals.

What you're willing to tolerate becomes the standards you must implement. **Standards are the actions linked to the thoughts you have related to your goals.**

Creating goals without creating corresponding standards is a waste of time. Your standards must be even more intentional than the goals you create. Think of your goals as the byproducts and results of your standards. Conversely, when you put the proper standards in place, you have a much better chance of achieving your goals.

The other thing is **you can't always control the outcome of your goals.** You will fail at achieving some. And you should. For goals to be meaningful, they must be difficult and challenging. However, **you can control your standards** because they are internal and rest entirely on you and how much you're willing to invest.

With that distinction made, you already have a sense of why goals are important. But, in my opinion, some of the thinking about goals and how to create meaningful and achievable goals for your life is entirely wrong.

Keep It Simple and Flexible

There are thousands and thousands of people out there who happily want to give you a system of creating goals. Here's the problem with that: One system doesn't fit everyone's needs.

That is because every one of us processes information differently. You are a unique product of your past experiences,

education, thoughts, gifts, shortcomings, and relationships.
A system does not fit everyone's process for creating goals.

Some people think visually. Others rely on auditory input as a
primary way to process information. Many people prefer a
tactile approach, with the need to literally touch their goals,
which is a more kinesthetic approach. If you've ever gone to a
car dealership to test drive the car of your dreams, you know
what I mean.

Most of us blend these and other approaches to varying
degrees in ways that reflect how we've been conditioned to
process information. That's why it's impossible to create a
goal-setting system that works effectively for 7 billion people on
planet Earth.

The other reason I believe many systems don't work is that
they're often too complicated. Elite performers, CEOs, and
other highly motivated, results-driven people don't have the
time or the inclination to dive into elaborate ways to
create goals.

The right way to approach setting your goals is to keep to a
simple plan of attack. I'm going to give you a flexible way to do
that so that it makes sense for *you*, no matter who you are. It's
not a system. It's a loose framework you can adapt to execute
actions in the most direct way that works best for you.

Creating Goals in Your Peak State

You can only create your best goals when you're at your peak
state. This state occurs when your mind and body are

functioning optimally together. Breaking it down further, think of your thoughts as your conscious mind and your body as your subconscious mind. When your conscious and your subconscious minds work in congruency, you have a powerful force that multiplies and heightens your peak state.

I refer to our body as our subconscious mind because too often, we only focus on our thoughts when it comes to creating our goals. Our thoughts are what puts us in a conscious state, giving us what we believe to be the right frame of mind to reach our goals. However, we don't realize that **for our mind to function optimally, our body must also function optimally**. Many people don't pay attention to their body when setting goals, and in this way, it becomes a subconscious mind.

When we don't put our subconscious mind in a prime state, we're not using all the available tools we have. Unless we tap into all these tools, there's no way our goals will best meet our needs. When these tools are in sync, **even when your conscious mind isn't actively working on your goals, your subconscious mind will keep pushing forward**.

Here's a critical point to remember: **Your mind always moves to what it is the most familiar with. When both your conscious and subconscious minds are engaged on your behalf, you are working on your goals *all the time*.** That's why this concept is so powerful. It's also why attaching compelling reasons to your goals is critical for success.

Compelling Reasons Drive Your Goals

Compelling reasons will give you the energy and resiliency to push through the difficult times so that you can reach your goals. **Compelling reasons translate into goals you're passionate about.**

Goals are all about change. That's why **your goals need to challenge you.** If they aren't challenging, then they won't change you. All you're doing is wasting your time. It's not compelling enough to say you'd like to raise $10,000 for your favorite charity because it would be a nice thing to do. Make it emotional! **The more emotional you make your compelling reasons, the more energy and resiliency you will attach to it.** And that means you're more likely to raise that $10,000.

For example, you need to set in your mind that raising that money will give children a place to go after school . . . something you never had as a child. Or put researchers one step closer to curing the disease your mom passed away from. Maybe that money can make a difference by paying for badly needed supplies at a battered women's shelter.

When I was younger, I had some heart problems. I started thinking about all the things I would miss if I passed away early in life. But the one image that caused me to make changes in my life was the vision I had of not being able to walk my daughter Bella down the aisle on her wedding day. I can't even begin to convey the emotional impact that had on me. Armed with that compelling reason, I started going to the gym, eating better, reducing my stress, and adopted an overall healthier lifestyle.

It's not simply a matter of being more disciplined or more driven. There needs to be an emotional component linked to your goal. That's the compelling motivation that keeps goals from become lethargic burdens.

As you create your goals, decide the "who, what, and why" reasons for what you're about to do. If you aren't fired up, then you'll have a difficult time fighting off the distractions that will try to dislodge you from your goal. Make your compelling reason your suit of armor to stave off these kinds of attacks.

Many goal-setting systems also encourage you to create goal categories. **Don't do it!** You have one life. There's no need to complicate it by categorizing them as finance, faith, fitness, or family goals. **Keep it simple.** Why burden yourself by complicating goals designed to make your life easier and better? When you create a single list, the only thing to keep in mind is whether you're creating a **momentum-building goal** or a **stretch, life-altering goal.**

Momentum-building goals are easier to hit. As the name suggests, they build momentum in your life. They're **shorter-term with a more immediate payoff**. You get a reward you can build on. Stringing enough of these together is a lot like gathering speed going downhill. The only caution here is to make sure that these types of goals are still meaningful and challenging.

Life-altering goals are harder to hit. You raise the bar on these with the idea that **they will produce a bigger payoff and result in bigger growth in you**. They take longer—sometimes years—to accomplish.

The two can be linked together. Let's use a very common goal as an example: losing weight. Start with your compelling reason, which is not to die prematurely because you're fat. A momentum-building goal is losing 2 pounds a week, or 8–10 pounds a month. If you set your standards the right way by eating the proper foods and exercising regularly, this is a short-term goal that's very doable.

If you're grossly overweight, you may set a life-altering goal of losing 100 pounds or more. The only way you'll do that is by hitting all your shorter, momentum-building goals. You can't lose 100 pounds if you don't first lose 2 pounds. Right?

Goethe understood this relationship when he said, "*It is not enough to take steps which may some day lead to a goal; each step must be itself a goal and a step likewise.*"

Finally, **when you design a goal, you carve out space in your brain that didn't exist before**. That space needs to be nurtured. You have to figure out what resources you'll need to help reach that goal. Is there a book you should read? A person you need to connect with? Maybe there's a place you need to visit or an activity you need to perform. Fill that space with the right tools to accomplish your goal, or you risk starving your goal into failure.

Nevertheless, you can have all your compelling reasons and resources in place, but if you don't think you deserve the goal you've set, you will struggle.

Goals and Self-Worth

If you don't believe you're worthy of a particular outcome, you're self-sabotaging, and you'll never produce a result greater than what you think you are worthy of. Think of it as pulling on both sides of the rope in a tug of war. Even if you win, you lose.

You must build two things into your thinking as you create your goals:

1. Ways to increase your faith in yourself.
2. Ways to increase your identity when you look in the mirror.

Both are integral parts of your self-worth. Unless you're confident in who you are and what you deserve, you'll limit yourself in the goals you think you deserve.

You must be aware and smart enough not to undermine your efforts. **As you believe, so too will you achieve.** Your conscious and your subconscious can be great allies. But if they're not working together, they can be the mental landmines that blow up in your face.

Using Positive Energy to Create Your Best Goals

Many people live with chaos, angst, anxiety, and suffering every day. Under this burden, they react and respond to these mental states to escape. When you create goals under these circumstances, you're reacting to your conditions instead of taking the reins and designing the life you want.

When you respond and react, you're moving away from something to avoid it instead of moving toward something better because you want it. **You need to set goals only when you're operating out of your imagination and dreams instead of out of your history and fears.**

The next obvious question is, "How can I do this?"

To design your goals, you need to lock out external factors and influences. With so much on our plates every day, this is a challenge. One way to prep your mind is to ask yourself this question: Would the quality of my goals and outcomes improve significantly if I created those goals operating under a state of confidence, strength, and bliss or operating out of a mindset of fear, failure, and depression?

Better goals create better outcomes. And better goals are created when you shed the negatives in your life while deciding what you want to accomplish. Again, there's no fancy formula here. I want you to keep it simple. Remember to create goals in your peak state.

To find your peak state, physically get your body moving. Go for a walk or a run. Hit the gym. Ride a bike. Take a swim or do some jumping jacks. When you do this, you're creating the energy I talked about at the beginning of this chapter. That energy generates endorphins that are released when you put your body in motion. The endorphins unleash your peak state, and **your peak state plugs into your best creative state**.

In your best creative state, you're able to see things differently. You imagine possibilities, and the adrenaline drives the confidence you need to develop your absolute best goals. When you generate this energy, it's transferred into your goals.

I told you goals are a form of energy. Now you know what fuels that energy.

After you've created your best goals, one of the keys to realizing them is by repeating them often. **When you repeat your goals, you fill your mind with thoughts your mind needs to help you accomplish your goals.** For maximum effectiveness, repeat your goals to yourself when you're in a peak state as well. To create congruency between your mind and body—your conscious state and subconscious state—you must repeat your goals in the same state you created them in. If you don't, there's a chance your mind will reject the goals. Your brain and your body should be in sync.

Engage a variety of tools to help you repeat your goals in your peak state. Use your cellphone, pictures, notes, daily appointments, or whatever tools you think are appropriate to reinforce repetition.

Also, the best way to create your goals is to create them in multiple timeframes. Lots of people wait until January 1st every year to do this. I can't even begin to tell you how lazy and inefficient that is. By contrast, **elite performers create and review goals several times a day.**

To design your goals instead of responding to circumstances in your life, **create goals hourly, daily, weekly, monthly, yearly, and even three and five years out**. The best set of goals have hybrid timeframes. That means you're working on goals with a sense of urgency (momentum goals) and long-term goals (stretch, life-altering goals) all the time.

Placed squarely in front of you, these blended timeframes make it easier to get into the habit of repeating your goals regularly. This is how you anchor your goals to your conscious mind. When you anchor goals in your conscious mind, your subconscious mind automatically kicks in, and your brain goes to work on your behalf.

How I Create Goals

How you create goals is going to be unique to you. However, I wanted to share with you how I create goals so you can get a better sense of how all the thoughts and strategies above fold into a practical example.

I would never presume to tell you precisely how you should create your goals. You must find a way that works best for you.

Your process will be different from everyone else, and that's the best way to ensure you create goals that work for you.

For me, every year, I come up with a one-word strategy that serves as an over-arching theme for my goals. This reflects what my priorities are and where I'm at in my life. Some of the words I've used in the past are relentless, faith, resilience, love, caring, and gratitude. Once I decide on that word, I step into that person. My goals remain unique, but this one word quietly drives my process in the background. I repeat that word all year long.

With this word in mind, and after putting myself in a peak mental state, **I start my goal setting with a mental flood.** It's exactly what it sounds like. First, I turn off the part of my brain that thinks I can't do something. Then, I see myself as a child on Christmas Eve, and I make a list of all the gifts I want to receive. I do this for four minutes. No editing. No throttling back. I write down everything that comes to mind. I give myself permission to empty my brain of all my desires, big and small.

While I'm doing this, I get up and move around. I make sure my blood is flowing. I remain in my peak state and create a strong internal energy flow. Once I have a single master list, I do several things to lock in this set of goals.

After I confirm that I have a compelling reason, **I drill down to ensure the goals I have are specific. Generalities don't work.** My brain, and yours, can't work effectively processing generic ideas. **A brain works best when frontloaded with detailed and precise pieces of information.**

I wouldn't say, "I want to get in shape and lose some weight so I'll feel better." Those are empty words and wishes. Instead, if losing weight is my goal, I zero in on the exact waist size I want, precisely how many pounds I want to lose, what I want my cholesterol and blood pressure readings to be, and so on.

Being vague gets in your mind's way. **Being specific means being accountable.** There's no wiggle room. In business, it's not enough to say I want to make more money. I need to come up with an exact amount. This is why I decided I wanted to make $1 million before I turned 30. **Part of the specificity of goals must include a date or a deadline.** Otherwise, it is little more than an open-ended wish.

Next, I decide who I want to help me be accountable for this goal. It might be my wife, my business partner, or my pastor. But **for my goal to work, I have to share what it is.** There's undeniable power in telling someone. **Discipline and accountability lead to ascension and dominance.**

With these things locked into place, I start to work on my goals. Part of this involves reading and visualizing my goals often. Sometimes this can be several times a day. **I've found that the most effective form of repetition is to repeat my goals out loud.** There's an added layer of impact when auditory senses are engaged.

Visualizing is critical, too. How you visualize is up to you. Some people use dream boards and photos. Others put written lists on mirrors, in their bathroom, or cars. Personally, I like to visualize in my mind. That's how I think. And it's what works best for me. Experiment with what works best for you.

The other part of repetition is that I say things I genuinely mean. Some goal-setting systems require you to act as if you've already accomplished a particular goal. Do this, and you're only lying to yourself. You'll knock your mind out of sync. Don't say, "I've got a million dollars," when you're not there yet.

I've found that repetition is hard for a lot of people. Personally, the way I do it is that I include my goals in my prayers, and I pray every day. Others meditate daily, and this is another great way to visualize goals as well. **Repetition is also easier when it's done at the same time every day.** For me, I like repeating my goals in the morning when I first wake up and at night just before I go to bed.

Repetition also engages the reticular activating system, or RAS. The RAS is the mental muscle that filters things into your awareness that are important to you and filters out things that are not. You can read more about the RAS in Chapter 2.

Finally, one last thing that I include when setting goals is that **I create an expectation that I am going to reach that goal.** Have you ever noticed that the goals you expect to happen are the ones you seem to hit time and time again? Expectation creates a positive framework that brings forward the tools and resources necessary to succeed. When your brain expects you to be successful, it goes to work putting solutions much closer in reach so that you can take full advantage at all times.

As a One More Thinker, you need goals in your life. When you craft them the right way, they will challenge you, energize you, and bring passion and focus to everything you do.

10

One More Higher Standard

*Of all the judgments we make through life, none are more
important than the estimate we place on ourselves according to
our own internal standards.*

—Denis Waitley

I'VE GOT A MIND-BLOWING REVELATION FOR
YOU. There's a very high probability you're not going to
reach your goals.

But here is some great news. You're absolutely guaranteed to
get your standards. Yep, that's the real truth.

Fortunately, goals and standards are two sides of the same
coin. They are inextricably linked together. That means **if you**

125

want the best possible chance of reaching your goals, you need to adjust your standards, and reaching your goals will become almost automatic. Here's how.

The Difference Between Goals and Standards

Many people I meet confuse goals and standards, often mistaking them as the same thing. They are not! Before you can achieve your goals, you must understand the role standards play and why they're so important.

Here's the key difference. Goals start out as thoughts. They are desirable outcomes that take root in your mind. Your brain either confirms these goals or they pass as fleeting thoughts. **When you decide you want to achieve your goals, you create standards as a means of taking those thoughts and applying actions to them.** Think of standards as the performance benchmarks you're willing to tolerate. Standards are the actions that propel you toward your goals. **Goals effectively become byproducts of how you approach your standards.** Goals without standards are empty. Goals without standards are useless.

The world constantly tells you to review and upgrade your goals, which you should be doing. But the secret is to constantly review and upgrade your standards. You need to evaluate what you're willing to tolerate and not tolerate.

What Are You Willing to Tolerate?

When you set a goal, you must decide if you can tolerate the standards that are essential to reach your goal. Tolerance doesn't apply only to the things you need to do to move your life forward. Your tolerance level can apply to many different areas, such as your existing relationships, leadership, and business dealings.

Right now, can you tolerate the business results you're currently getting? Can you tolerate the amount of money you currently make? Can you tolerate the amount of bliss or passion you currently experience? If you can, you're going to keep getting them. It's only when you decide that you can no longer tolerate the treatment you're getting in a relationship, or the business results that you're getting, that you can change them. It's only when you decide you can no longer tolerate the amount of money you're making that you'll begin to move forward to your goal of making more money. **If you're willing to tolerate something, that's probably what you're going to get.**

If you don't change your standards, then your goals are irrelevant.

Many people fail or are miserable because they set standards that are too low for how they want to be treated. **If you don't establish what your standards are and clearly define them, other people will act to undermine them simply because they aren't clear about what is acceptable to you and what is not.**

Sometimes, this downward push can unintentionally come from well-meaning people in your life who may not even be aware they're doing this to you. For example, if high standards and boundaries don't exist between two people, the relationship will be troubled, and often fail.

Your relationship standards must be clearly defined and mutually agreed upon. Also, **never tolerate treatment less than what you're worthy of.** Set standards in your relationship with your spouse, boyfriend/girlfriend, business relationships, or anyone else in your life. **Make those standards consistent with your self-worth.**

In business, an organization without high standards is an organization that is out of control. It's an organization not performing at peak capacity. As competitive as business is, that's a recipe for failure. In your business, can every employee tell you what the organization's goals are and what the standards are to achieve those business goals? And just as important, can they live up to them? **The greatest companies and the dynastic sports teams always set the highest standards.**

Where You Find Your Standards

You already have standards that define your life. Understanding where those standards came from is one of the steps to leveling up and creating higher standards that will lead you to change. Your standards reflect the people you work with, your parents, friends, family members, your church, social media, news media, and the books you read.

You have other tribal influences as well. If you're an athlete, you idolize stars like Simone Biles, Mia Hamm, LeBron James, Mike Trout, or Patrick Mahomes. Techies identify with Steve Jobs, Mark Zuckerberg, and Jeff Bezos. Intellectuals are moved by great thought and religious leaders like Dr. Martin Luther King, Jr., Mahatma Gandhi, Ayn Rand, Rick Warren, or Brené Brown.

And you can never underestimate music's power through artists like Michael Jackson, Beyoncé, Adele, Taylor Swift, John Mayer, Post Malone, or Ed Sheeran.

You may have even been influenced by one-off casual conversations you've had with strangers.

By our nature, we are social creatures. We need input. We seek validation in our relationships. Most of us enjoy belonging to a variety of groups of like-minded people. We like exchanging ideas and learning new things that grow and shape our perceptions. These perceptions influence our beliefs about our world, our community, our family, and most importantly, our own being. You can't turn off these types of interactions. You'd wither and die. But you can **be more aware of how these interactions shape what you think and how that defines you as a person**. Make it a point to understand how they impact you from a behavioral, moral, ethical, and Godly perspective.

Think of Your Brain as a Blender

Once you're exposed to different ideas, your brain takes all that input, whether you agree with it or not, and blends those thoughts to create something new. You may completely reject new notions on the surface, but subconsciously, your brain processes things over time. And you might change your way of thinking, perhaps in a way that leads you to higher and more enlightened standards.

The incoming information you receive daily is inevitable. **To activate the changes meant for you, there must be a conscious decision to take only what you think is valuable and apply it in a thoughtful way to create your unique standards.**

If you are lazy and go with the standards of the people, places, groups, and media you're in proximity with, you'll get the same things as everyone else. That isn't the way to your best life.

Activating to a Higher Standard

Are you happy with the amount of money you're currently making? Perhaps you've been stuck in a job that has paid you $75,000 a year for the past three years. You tell yourself, "I want to make $100,000 next year." That's your goal.

The question now becomes, "How will I get there?" And that's where standards come into play. **Standards are the specific set of actions you must take to achieve your goal.**

In this case, you might need to increase the number of calls you make to clients or take business classes that add to your value, making you a more attractive candidate for a promotion. You may need to come to work earlier, stay later, put in some time on Saturdays, or find a new job that pays you what you think you're worth.

Standards are most valuable when they are precise.

Make 20 calls more per week to clients. Take classes that will lead you to your Masters' degree in 18 months. Commit to working six hours every Saturday and staying two hours later three days a week. These actions become your standards for reaching your goal.

Unfortunately, many people never get beyond dreaming about their goals. Even if there's a strong desire to achieve a goal they've set, they don't want to pay the price for reaching that goal. **In all parts of your life, when it comes to goals and standards, they must be aligned to find harmony. That harmony will breed success.**

Goals without standards are just a bunch of rudderless thoughts and words. They're only unattached desires that will never materialize unless you pair them with the right standards. If you've created goals and fallen short, it's because your standards are not congruent with your goals.

Here's something else that is truly liberating: **When you set the right standards that match your goals, your life becomes much less stressful.** Your goals, while important, become secondary. That may sound a bit counterintuitive, but it's the truth.

For example, if you want to build a championship team, what are the preparation standards you're willing to tolerate? What are the execution standards you're willing to tolerate?

Coach Nick Saban is the greatest college football coach of all time. His teams have won more than 80 percent of the 300-plus games he's coached. During the 2020 season, he won his seventh national championship, despite contracting Covid-19 mid-season. Even more impressive, his Crimson Tide rolled to an undefeated 13-0 season along the way.

Coach Saban sets a different kind of standard than most other coaches. Those coaches create the standard of, "We'll practice this until we get it right." Coach Saban sets the standard of, "We'll practice this until we can't get it wrong."

That's next-level thinking and a next-level standard. It's also a championship standard. The difference is so subtle but it separates the greatest of all time from the rest of the world.

Nine Ways to Set a Higher Standard

Setting clear and defined higher standards is personal and unique to you. But there are some universal principles you can apply that will ensure you create quality higher standards, no matter what your goals are.

Here are some things to consider:

1. **Understand your "why."** Unless you're clear on your motivation, you won't develop optimal standards for your goal. It's a lot different saying, "I want to lose 50 pounds because it might be a good idea," instead of "I want to lose 50 pounds because my back hurts, my doctor says I have high blood pressure, I'm borderline diabetic, and I may not live to see my grandchildren." The stronger and more specific your reasons are for doing something, the more likely you'll stick with your standards.

2. **Break down a higher standard into detailed and achievable steps.** Don't say, "I'm gonna get up and run a little while, then lift some weights." Be intentional, meticulous, and specific.

   Tell yourself, "I'm going to run eight miles three days a week, work with a trainer to create an optimal strength training routine that I'll do five days a week, and I'll change my diet to a lean protein and plant-based menu."

3. **Be honest with yourself.** If you take on the workout regimen above and you're 55 years old and weigh 350 pounds, not only are you setting yourself up for failure, you're setting yourself up for a 911 ambulance ride.

   Don't let your ego run your mind when it comes to setting realistic goals and standards. Start at a place that makes sense for you. You can always upgrade your goals and standards once you start making progress. Be measured and transparent with yourself when developing your standards.

4. **Get help in areas where you're weak.** Find a workout buddy. Enlist a seasoned business mentor. Listen to motivational tapes and podcasts. Surround yourself with like-minded people on like-minded journeys. Do whatever it takes to fortify your efforts.

   There are going to be days and periods where you'll waver. You'll want to give up. That's normal. You may question if your goal is worth it. You may tell yourself that your standards are too high. Welcome to the human condition.

   This is where mental discipline comes in. Revisit your original motivation. Understand what influences are holding you back, and then eliminate them if possible.

   Well-intentioned friends, family, and business associates can be your biggest enemies because they are also your greatest allies. Like it or not, you care what they think, good and bad. They're part of your inner circle and will constantly influence your thoughts and your actions. It's up to you to filter the messages that are positive and meaningful to you. Don't be swayed to a lesser outcome simply because of familiarity.

   Worthy goals and corresponding standards are not supposed to be easy to reach. If your willpower wavers, redouble your efforts and give yourself credit for being smart enough to recognize that you'll have to work harder as part of your process.

5. **Use technology to set and maintain your new standards.** Not so long ago, self-improvement gurus preached that you needed to write down your goals, look in the bathroom mirror, and repeat those goals every day. We've come a long way since then. To optimize the possibility of being

successful, tap into technology to help you set and maintain your standards.

Use your cellphone or computer to create a video of your goals and standards. Talk to yourself. Do it when you're in a focused, high-energy state. That way, when you play it back, you'll be watching yourself in a peak state every time.

Unlike only writing down your goals and standards, you'll get the added boost of auditory and visual stimulation sent to your brain. Your brain's synaptic plasticity will improve. When this happens, your brain is better able to flex and adapt, creating enhanced avenues for learning.

You are watching the person you want to be. Think of it as You 2.0.

6. **Give dedicated thought to the relationship between your goal and your standard.** Venus and Serena Williams didn't learn to play world-class tennis by going out after school a couple of times a week and playing a friendly match here and there. Both women became highly accomplished tennis players because they spent thousands of hours honing their skills, working on every little part of their game to eventually become legends in the game. They created standards commensurate with their goal of being the best tennis players in the world.

When your standard does not match what's required to meet your goal, you won't be properly motivated. If you set your standards beneath your capabilities, you won't feel challenged, and you'll lose interest.

Low standards produce low results. So why bother?

7. **Forget perfection.** This is an absolute killer. Perfection is the lowest standard there is. And realistically, perfection doesn't exist. If you want to frustrate yourself and give up,

assume that you must be perfect. Even the Williams sisters have lost plenty of matches along the way.

Perfection is also boring! It's our flaws that make us interesting. Human. And relatable. Everybody has flaws. And those who think they don't have any are the ones who have the biggest flaws of all.

8. **Don't overthink it.** Be diligent and thorough. But for goodness sake's get over yourself and get your butt in gear. I've seen thousands of people become their own worst enemy due to overthinking. I've seen so many people have great ideas for incredible businesses, only to tinker, dabble, focus on the minutiae, and fizzle out before they even reach the starting line.

Thinking is good. Overthinking is bad!

9. **Set standards to please yourself.** I covered this already, but it bears repeating simply because we're hard-wired to please others. Be selfish when it comes to developing your standards. This is your journey. This does not belong to anyone else. It's personal. Keep it that way, or you're just going to waste time, wind up with a big mess you don't buy into, and end up in worse shape than when you started.

I love Rick Pitino's take on this: *"Set higher standards for your own performance than anyone around you, and it won't matter whether you have a tough boss or an easy one. It won't matter whether the competition is pushing you hard because you'll be competing with yourself."*

Raising Your Standards Is an Ongoing Process

Nobody knows better than you what your standards should be. That said, developing standards isn't always an easy proposition.

If you're trying to break out and do something new, you might not have all the tools or knowledge you need to accurately assess what standards you'll need to develop to reach your goals.

The good news is, they aren't set in stone. People often create standards they think are in line with what they need to reach their goals. However, as they gain experience and other variables come into play, these dynamics can create a need to dial up to a higher standard.

Your standards should be appropriately challenging. You will grow and change along the way. **So, you should review your goals and your higher standards regularly. When you've mastered a standard and met your goal, adjust upward.**

If you've been diligent in your efforts and something is starting to feel "easy," you'll know. Maybe it's time to set a different goal with different standards once you've accomplished what you want. **But for a remarkable difference in your life, consider leveling up by creating a higher standard that will propel you to an even more worthy goal that builds on what you've already done.**

Also, **it's unhealthy to compare yourself or your standards to others.** This is your journey and yours alone. Keep it that way! You have no clue what somebody else is going through, even when they tell you. *Especially* when they tell you. You're only going to hear what they want you to hear. When you compare, you're also tempted to adjust your standards downward to align with someone else's standards. That's unacceptable. **It's human nature to compare, but I'm telling you now, don't do it!**

Consider the alternative. Suppose you compare your standards to someone else's, and you discover their standards are incredibly high when stacked against yours. In that case, you may be setting yourself up for a big psychological disappointment. It's a waste of time and doesn't do one thing to move you closer to your desired outcomes. **The only person you should be comparing yourself to is you.**

The Consequences of Higher Standards

Change creates consequences. Setting higher standards creates consequences. **When One More thinkers set a higher standard, you'll experience consequences, good and bad.**

The good is obvious. When your goals are aligned with your higher standards, you'll enjoy a fuller and more blissful life. When you repeat this process in several areas of your life, you'll experience a powerful transformation. Not only will you treat yourself better, you'll treat others better, too. Likewise, others will understand that you have a higher expectation of how you want to be treated, and most will honor that expectation and treat you with added respect.

However, **some people in your circle will become jealous of your discipline and success.** If they continue to doubt you, remain jealous, or if they can't see that they can share and celebrate your success, you need to reconsider your relationship with those people. They'll get over it soon enough. Or, as harsh as it may sound, you may need to let them go.

As you develop higher standards, you'll also enjoy more resilience. You'll bounce back from setbacks quicker. Your higher standards will become habits and replace the lesser standards that used to guide you. **Even if you don't fully succeed, you'll still fail at a higher level and land at a higher baseline.** Once you dust yourself off, you'll be in a better place to move on to new goals and other higher standards.

Setting higher standards in your life is not easy. But consider the alternative: If you aim low, set unworthy goals, and create uninspired standards, you'll end up living a life far below what you're capable of and far below what you deserve.

11

One More Impossibility Thinkers and Possibility Achievers

*One's philosophy is not best expressed in words; it is expressed
in the choices one makes. In the long run, we shape our lives
and we shape ourselves. The process never ends until we die.
And, the choices we make are ultimately our own responsibility.*
—Eleanor Roosevelt

THE FUNDAMENTAL PHILOSOPHY OF ONE
MORE combines both the acts of thinking and doing.

To fully realize your best life, it's not enough to think about
what you want to do. Your thinking can be pristine and spot on.

Unless you put actions to those thoughts, you're not going anywhere in life. One More thinkers must also be One More doers. To frame the marriage of these two elements the right way, I want you to become an impossibility thinker *and* a possibility achiever.

Learn to Think and Do Rich

If you're serious about improving your life, one of the best books on the subject is Napoleon Hill's *Think and Grow Rich*. Generations of successful businesspeople, entrepreneurs, entertainers, athletes, and those of more modest means and goals worldwide have gleaned valuable ideas and been inspired to next levels of greatness after reading this seminal book.

As a One More thinker, you should read Hill's book if you haven't done so already. It has several great tools to break through barriers and become a more dynamic impossibility thinker who dares to dream about things that most others think of as impossible.

Your dreams equal your riches. Maybe your dream is to live on a ranch and raise cattle in Wyoming. Or to launch a company that provides clean drinking water to impoverished areas of the world. You may dream about making a living playing music or acting and bringing joy to others as an entertainer.

I have profound respect for both Napoleon Hill and *Think and Grow Rich*. My only issue with the book is that I don't think it goes far enough as a high-performance cornerstone for contemporary times. When it was written in 1937, the world was a very different place. America was deep in the midst of the Depression. Vast numbers of people were out of work and starving. Problems in Europe were starting to foreshadow an ominous future of what would become World War II. Americans needed hope. Napoleon Hill, inspired by a suggestion from Andrew Carnegie, delivered it to them.

More than 80 years after it first debuted, *Think and Grow Rich* has sold more than 15 million copies and is considered a must-read for anyone who wants to succeed in any line of work. **All the principles in *Think and Grow Rich* are critical for success.** They're worth mentioning because they're still valid and powerful strategies today.

Those principles are:

> Thoughts Are Things
>
> Desire
>
> Faith
>
> Autosuggestion
>
> Specialized Knowledge
>
> Imagination
>
> Organized Planning
>
> Decision
>
> Persistence
>
> Power of the Master Mind
>
> The Mystery of Sex
>
> Transmutation
>
> The Subconscious Mind
>
> The Brain
>
> The Sixth Sense

If you read the book, you'll see that all of these concepts relate primarily to thoughts. But you don't get rich simply by thinking. **You get rich by doing. More specifically, you get rich, highly productive, or happier when your thoughts and your actions are congruent.**

Although one of Hill's most famous thoughts is about action, "The man who does more than he is paid for will soon be paid for more than he does," his book doesn't go far enough. You must marry actions to your thoughts if you want to reach your goals.

Your thoughts are the starting point of your dreams, and you owe it to yourself to aim high with your dreams. The sad part is **many people never get beyond dreaming.** Their dreams end in their thoughts. That unrealized potential to do something great and be happy can be maddening.

Dreams are the essence of impossibility thinking. You must be able to dream to plant the seeds of what you think you can do in life.

It's when you combine that impossibility thinking with intentional actions aimed squarely at achieving your dreams that you become a possibility achiever.

Think of your dreams as challenges that live inside of you. You lose nothing by challenging yourself this way. It's healthy, and I strongly encourage you to think long and hard about what will help you find your version of riches in life.

But don't stop there. To realize what life has in store, you must **think and do rich**. Dreams and thoughts without accompanying actions will only depress and frustrate you.

One More thinkers understand this and implement an updated corollary of Newton's Third Law of Motion. You know the original law, which states, "For every action, there is an equal and opposite reaction." In this case, that updated corollary is, "For every thought, there is an equal and complementary action." **Thoughts and actions act as a pair.** Borrowing more from Newton's Law, One More thinkers also understand that "the size of the thoughts you have should equal the force of the actions you should take."

You can't always control your thoughts. That's the beauty of the human brain at work. There are no wrong dreams in your head. **The problem is that it's impossible to measure your thoughts or the thoughts of someone else. However, you can control what you do, and what you do is measurable.**

For example, if you work out at the gym and you want to increase your arm strength, two sets of eight reps on the dumbbell curls can become three sets of 10 reps. If you want better cardio fitness, 30 minutes on a treadmill can become 45 minutes. Instead of working out three days a week, you go to the gym five days a week.

Measuring your progress by measuring your actions makes you a possibility achiever. Are there risks and costs associated with taking action? Of course, there are. But the risks and costs associated with not taking action are a lot more. **Inaction stifles progress and kills personal growth.** Your time is finite and limited, so why would you continue to sit still instead of engaging in the life you are meant to lead?

Become an Impossibility Thinker and a Possibility Achiever

Great philosophers throughout history have long understood the link between thoughts and actions.

The Greek philosopher Epictetus encouraged his followers to ". . . *not worry about anything outside of your control. The only things you command are your thoughts and actions. We choose our response. Stop aspiring to be anyone other than your own best self, for that does fall within your control.*"

1 John 3:18 tells us, "*Let us not love with words or speech but with actions in truth.*"

Mahatma Gandhi is one of many who voiced a version of the following:

Your beliefs become your thoughts,
Your thoughts become your words,
Your words become your actions,
Your actions become your habits,
Your habits become your values,
Your values become your destiny.

Mark Twain kept it simpler but equally effective when he wrote, "*Actions speak louder than words but not nearly as often.*"

The concept of being an impossibility thinker and a possibility achiever is not new. The problem is that putting these two ideas together is often overlooked. Procrastination, denial, or fear are common reasons why thinkers get stuck thinking and don't move on to doing.

Lots of guys will see an attractive woman and think about asking her out. But only a few will break through their fear or procrastination and have the guts to follow through. Ever see a beautiful woman on a very average man's arm and ask yourself, "How did he do that!?" **He did it because he's a One More impossibility thinker and possibility achiever.**

Babies are remarkable human beings. Take the simple act of a baby learning to walk. All his or her life, a baby has only known crawling. They see other humans upright and walking around, and they begin to imagine a world where they break through the impossibility of standing upright on their own. At first, they'll grab onto a coffee table or a couch and pull themselves up. They will fall. There will be a few tears, bumps, and bruises. Eventually, that baby is going to stand upright, put one foot in front of the other, and much to mom and dad's delight, start walking like it's old hat. It takes babies hundreds of hours of practice from the moment of first learning how to stand to walk unassisted. It's a monumental achievement worthy of every parent's celebration.

If a baby can do it, you can become an impossibility thinker and possibility achiever, too. **You must be willing to dream big, take a chance, set your barriers aside, and do it anyway.** Whether it's learning how to ballroom dance, day trade stocks, or set a goal of headlining at Carnegie Hall, put your subconscious to work, and soon enough, your actions will propel you toward your goals.

Watching Your Silent Movie

If you show me your actions and behaviors, I can show you how you think. That's because **what you do is a reflection of how you're thinking**. However, what you're thinking isn't always a reflection of what you do.

This is important because once you understand how the relationship between a person's thoughts and actions works, you can predict their behavior. I'm sure you'll agree that's a powerful tool to have at your disposal. Here are several examples of what I mean.

I can't tell if you're thinking about going on a diet to lose 40 pounds. But I can tell you what your body will look like based on how you eat and work out. Do you gorge late at night on cookies and ice cream? Or do you hit the gym or go for a run several days a week?

Several "tells" for a woman going on a first date with a man will reveal to her the kind of guy he is and whether she should carry the relationship forward. These aren't disqualifiers. But they are indicators. For example, does he open doors for you? If you're at a restaurant, how does he treat the hostess and the wait staff? Does he shut his phone off when he's with you? Or at the very least, apologize if he has to take an important phone call? **What many people call women's intuition could just be highly tuned observational note-taking.**

When you're sitting across the table from someone attempting to negotiate a big business deal, what does that person's body language tell you about their interest level? Are they anxious to wrap things up, or do they ask important questions to drill down to the deal's finer points? Do they try to grind you on every little detail, or do they understand the best deals are win-win and instead seek common ground?

In these situations, and most of your interactions with others, **what you do trumps how you think**. Your life isn't based on your thoughts. Your life is based on your actions. Show me what you do, and I'll tell you what you think. To illustrate this point, I've developed something I call **"Watching a Silent Movie."**

Suppose, in all your interactions with others, there was no sound. You had no choice but to make assumptions and decisions about others based only on what their actions were. In effect, no sound means you can't hear their thoughts. However, despite no sound, you can still see the outcome of their thoughts by how their Silent Movie plays out in front of you.

Here's another easy way to understand and test out "Watching a Silent Movie." The next time you're sitting on your couch at home, find a show you haven't watched before. Flip it on, but then mute the sound. Romantic comedies are an excellent genre to test out. Often, the plots are centered on hidden desires that reveal themselves over two hours. Play the game. Can you figure out the plot based on the action only?

You may already do this when a friend or family member calls you during a show you don't want to stop watching. You mute the television. You have a short chat, all the while eyeballing your show. Most of the time, when the call ends, there's no need to rewind. You just unmute and keep watching your show, never feeling like you missed a beat.

Alignment Is the Key

In life, **winning is all about how well you interact with others**. Trying to understand what's on someone's mind is a critical element for a positive outcome. Except, as I've mentioned, you can't always tell what other people are thinking. Yes, many people do tip their hand by talking too much. But just as many people hide their thoughts by being tight-lipped. In some cases, they'll even lie to you.

What works well in reading other people works well for you, too. **Alignment between your thoughts and your actions is essential for success.** Even though balancing thoughts and actions can be a challenge for many people, **alignment occurs when your thoughts manifest themselves in the actions**

you take. This is why the best of the best become impossibility thinkers *and* possibility achievers.

When you set high standards and take actions congruent with those standards that you've thought about, you'll enjoy success and bliss. As English philosopher and physician John Locke once said, *"I have always thought the actions of men the best interpreters of their thoughts."* With the seeds firmly planted in your brain, it is much easier to act a certain way if you are aligned.

I know positive thinkers who have won in life. But I also know many skeptical and pessimistic thinkers who have succeeded in life as well. I know some people with tremendous vision who have won and people with an equally big vision who have lost. I also know some people with limited vision who have succeeded. I know big and aggressive thinkers who have won and others who are conservative and risk-averse who have won as well.

There is no single way of thinking that causes people to be successful. But there is only one way of acting and behaving that can lead to extraordinary results: become a One More impossibility thinker and possibility achiever.

Reflecting on Martin Luther King, Jr. and *Strength to Love*

If you know anything about me, you know I believe **Martin Luther King, Jr. is one of the finest human beings who ever lived.** I look to him often, with reverence, and as a source of comfort and common sense. I want to share this passage from his collection of sermons, *Strength to Love*, because of its profound impact on me, and I hope it will have the same effect on you as well. There is no finer way to sum up the ongoing challenge of what it means to be an impossibility thinker and possibility achiever than these words:

> *One of the great tragedies of life is that men seldom bridge the gulf between practice and profession, between doing and saying. A persistent schizophrenia leaves so many of us tragically divided against ourselves.*
>
> *On the one hand, we proudly profess certain sublime and noble principles, but on the other hand, we sadly practice the very antithesis of these principles. How often are our lives characterised by a high blood pressure of creeds and an anaemia of deeds!*
>
> *We talk eloquently about our commitment to the principles of Christianity, and yet our lives are saturated with the practices of paganism. We proclaim our devotion to democracy, but we sadly practice the very opposite of the democratic creed. We talk passionately about peace, and at the same time we assiduously prepare for war. We make our fervent pleas for the high road of justice, and then we tread unflinchingly the low road of injustice.*
>
> *This strange dichotomy, this agonising gulf between the ought and the is, represents the tragic theme of man's earthly pilgrimage.*

12

One More Habit

Your net worth to the world is usually determined by what remains after your bad habits are subtracted from your good ones.

—Benjamin Franklin

SHOW ME YOUR HABITS, AND I'LL SHOW YOU YOUR LIFE.

I can predict with a high degree of accuracy the results you're going to achieve based on your habits because the outcomes in your life are directly related to your habits.

Your brain understands the importance of habits because it's an incredibly efficient organ. The brain's DNA is hard-wired to protect you by conserving mental energy whenever it can.

Saving energy means that reserves can be applied to other parts of your life where more brainpower is needed.

What does that have to do with habits?

Your brain is constantly trying to save energy.

This is an important point to understand because it directly relates to how to build and change habits, and why you even have habits in the first place.

Habits are a direct result of your brain subconsciously taking actions in a way to ensure that you'll use less energy to get a desired outcome. **With habits, your brain already knows what you need to do, and it switches to an autopilot mode,** much like setting a car on cruise control to create maximum fuel efficiency.

Think of how many times you've wakened in the morning and gone through your routine of grooming, getting dressed, and eating breakfast. If you have a set schedule, there's a good chance that most days, you've sleep-walked through all these tasks before fully realizing you're awake and ready to start your day. You know that jolt . . . the first moment of morning clarity, and it rarely strikes when you first wake up.

You got to that point in the day because your habits carried you through.

Here's the kicker. Several studies have shown that most of the actions you take are habits.

Some people drink two cups of coffee by 8 a.m. without fail. Other people eat lunch at precisely the same time every day. Golfers have an exacting routine when they swing a club, and people who go to the gym often do so on the same days of the week and do the same workouts every time.

Sometimes, these habits are even more specific and more routine, and we're even less aware of them. For example, most people either brush their teeth first or jump in the shower first to start their day. It never varies.

How about you? Which do you do first, and how often do you think about it?

Let's take it a step further.

We'll talk more about triggers further down in this chapter, but for now, when you step into the shower, the water is a trigger that starts a habit of what you do in the shower.

Do you start by shampooing your head? Do you grab a bar of soap and lather up your face and then the rest of your body? Do you routinely stand and just let the water run on your back for a minute while you're relaxing or starting to plan your day?

I'll bet there's a grooming sequence you go through every day and you don't think about, do you?

That's a prime example of how habits work.

When you get in your car to begin your work commute, turning the car on is a trigger that starts the habit of how you'll drive to work. You may adjust your mirrors, buckle your seatbelt, turn on your car radio, plug in a favorite podcast, and check your fuel level before putting your car into drive and pulling away from your home.

Your brain goes into habit mode because you've already driven to work so many times that your brain knows what to do with a lot less active thinking on your part.

That single trigger of starting your car initiates a habit that lasts for the duration of your commute to work, saving you a lot of brain energy in the process.

Countless types of activities are habits. You don't think about them. You just do them. And many times, those habits work out just fine for you.

But not always. Sometimes you develop bad habits, and they don't end up serving you well.

When that happens, if you want to change your life for the better, pay close attention to your habits and make changes that align with what you want out of life.

Be Intentional About Your Habits

Under pressure, you'll always move into a habitual mode in your brain. **Habits are reflexive.**

For example, if you want to maintain a high level of fitness, but you're in the habit of only going to the gym twice a week, and you sneak a lot of junk food into your diet, you're not going to achieve that goal.

If you want a close knit and happy family life, do you schedule a date night once a week with your spouse, or private time with your kids? Is there a recurring time in your home where you all gather as a family? Do you have the habit of eating at the dinner table together most nights?

Those types of habits are what creates a happy family life for you.

Perhaps you want more peace in your life, but you don't cultivate the habit of praying, meditating, or going to church. How will you calm your mind if you don't do the things you need to put you in a state of grace?

Or, if you want to be a great leader but don't actively apply critical principles of leadership in your work or personal life, you'll fail in those areas as well. **Getting fired up about living your life well each day is important but nowhere near as important as having good habits.**

Octavia Butler put it into perspective this way when she said, "*. . . forget inspiration. A habit is more dependable. Habits will sustain you whether you're inspired or not.*"

Contrary to what you believe and what you may have been told, **the biggest separator in life is not motivation or inspiration. It is the habits you create to get you through those days when you don't really feel like doing the things you need to do to be successful.**

What do you do when you're not feeling great? Or when it's not your best day? How do you make progress on your projects and goals at those times?

It's rituals and habits.

Motivation and inspiration come and go. But rituals and habits are constant.

Creating positive and effective habits will change your life. The good news is that this can take place with just a few simple steps. There's no need to over-complicate the process.

However, before you can learn how to do this, it's crucial to understand how habits are born, why we rely on them so much, and what happens inside of our brain when a habit kicks in.

The Science of Habits

When you understand how habits are created and why your brain uses them to benefit you, learning how to upgrade your habits makes more sense.

Life would be so much easier if we lived in a relaxed state all day long. Instead, often, we live with varying degrees of pressure and stress. This stress can be caused by anything such as paying bills, hitting a pressure shot in a game if you're a basketball player, having a disagreement with your spouse, or attending an important meeting with your boss or a big client.

On the one hand, you view these as normal parts of your life. However, in neurological terms, your brain does not distinguish between these events and treats them as threats. **When we perceive these threats, our brain flips a switch, moves out of thinking mode, and goes into a reflex mode.** We react and revert to what we know as a form of protection.

And what we know are our habits.

In biological terms, in response to a perceived threat, your hypothalamus activates and prompts your adrenal glands to release hormones, including adrenaline and cortisol. Adrenaline increases your heart rate, raises your blood pressure and energy levels. Cortisol is the body's primary stress hormone, and when it's activated, it releases glucose into the bloodstream. That triggers several bodily functions, including alarm systems in the regions of the brain that control mood, motivation, and fear.

Also, **when stress hits and you go into a habit mode, if you don't have the right habits in place, you'll sink into depression, despair, and fear**. When this repeatedly happens over a long period, it can lead to chronic anxiety, heart disease, sleep problems, weight gain, digestive problems, and memory and concentration degradation, among others.

By contrast, when you engage in positive habits that result in good outcomes, your body produces dopamine. Dopamine creates a sense of euphoria, and this euphoria dials your bodily systems back and conserves energy, which is what your brain naturally tries to do as much as possible.

If your habits involve confidence, passion, resilience, strength, and peace, you'll reflexively respond with those emotions when stress hits.

Dopamine pathways control the operations of the basal ganglia. Basal ganglia are located near the "base" or the bottom of the brain. This cluster of nuclei has extensive roles in the brain, including involvement in a variety of cognitive, emotional, and movement-related functions.

Here's how this all ties back to habits.

Brains can change and adapt as a result of experience. This is known as brain plasticity or neuroplasticity.

Neurons are the building blocks of the brain and nervous system. Neuroplasticity means they can be rewired, develop new pathways, and create new connections.

When basal ganglia engage in neuroplasticity, this is how new habits are created.

Neuroplasticity is what allows you to learn new things, enhance your existing cognitive capabilities, recover from strokes and traumatic brain injuries, and strengthen some brain functions that you've lost or are in decline.

Now, let's take this science and plug it into how you can develop One More new habit.

Trigger, Action, Prize

As a One More thinker, your goal is to create new habits that focus on releasing dopamine and minimize perceived threats that release adrenaline and cortisol. Keep in mind, habits are directly related to your emotions that are controlled by your basal ganglia where emotions emanate.

Whether you realize it or not, these habitual emotions control you. So, **when you reframe your emotions, you also reframe your habits**. Because habits make up so much of your life, you can make tremendous strides in all areas that you want to improve when you adjust your way of thinking and develop positive habits.

Creating new habits involves three steps: **The trigger, the action, and the prize**.

The Trigger

The keys to creating new habits are **intentional thought and repetition**.

To develop these things, the first thing you should do is make a list of the habits you'll need to reach a particular goal. Be specific and write them down.

For example, if your goal involves fitness, what are the habits you need to develop? What kind of exercise, eating, protein intake, and hydration habits would you need to accomplish this goal?

Then, list the habits that don't serve you well related to the goals you want to achieve. You can do this by starting with the emotions you gravitate to under times of stress. Do you get uptight, angry, fearful, tense up, or lose confidence? Those habitual emotions are going to dictate your actions.

As you do this, ask yourself, "When I'm under stress, will I achieve a better outcome if I'm filled with these negative emotions or more positive emotions, such as calmness, equanimity, and focus?"

Remember, your brain is constantly trying to find a way to conserve energy. It does this by minimizing the number of choices in your life and replacing them by hard-wiring habits into your subconscious mind.

When your brain perceives an action impacting you, it's triggered into a response. Your basal ganglia go to work to respond to this action. **Whenever possible, habits become the primary response to this trigger. That's why it's important to have proper habits already programmed into your brain.** A positive habitual response is more likely to produce a dopamine release.

The Action

The action you take is your response to the heightened state of alert you're confronted with.

Let's say you're a baseball player, and you step into the batter's box. Your body automatically treats this as an important situation and recognizes you need to execute this task at a high level.

It can't distinguish between playing a game or trying to escape a house that's on fire. It only understands that an external stimulus must be dealt with the best way your brain knows how to do it.

To the extent you've developed good habits as a batter, the more confidence you'll have when you step into the batter's box. And your brain and your body will react reflexively. In baseball parlance, you have a greater chance of being "locked in," giving you a higher probability you're going to hit the ball well.

Let me give you an example of what I often do when I'm working with athletes to help them change their habits and performance.

When you're a competitor, no matter what game you play, you're likely to hit a slump sooner or later. If you're a golfer, you're missing easy putts. If you're a basketball player, you're having trouble making free throws. If you're in sales, maybe you've missed a dozen closes in a row.

What do you do? You need to build a new habit.

How do you do that? The first thing you need to do is **build a new trigger**.

When I work with hitters in baseball, the first thing I'll do is have them change their trigger. This means the first thing they do when they step into the batter's box is to change the trigger that puts them into a habit mode. For example, instead of tapping the plate once before they get ready to swing, maybe they tap the plate three times. Perhaps I'll have them adjust their batting gloves a different way or take a different number of practice swings. Doing this triggers a new habit.

Although these may appear small and inconsequential, when you're intentional about doing them, you move out of the habit that was not serving you well and force your brain into a new thinking mode. **Small adjustments are triggers that create new habits** that can completely change a plate appearance.

Also understand that hard-wiring your brain to develop new pathways requires repetition. Creating the right actions to produce better habits involves practice. Lots and lots of practice!

You can't expect to do something once and have it become a habit. Depending on what you want to do or change, creating new habits can take several days up to several months to master.

That point was driven home by Mark Twain who once said, *"A habit cannot be tossed out the window; it must be coaxed down the stairs a step at a time."*

When you're patient and intentional, in most cases you can develop a new habit in about 30 days. But you can't be lazy about it. You must work hard, think about what you're doing, and where you want to get to before your new habit will become a reality.

The Prize

This is the payoff. **When you create a new habit and use it to accomplish a goal, you release dopamine. This dopamine tells your brain you want to do it again. The more dopamine your brain releases, the greater the intensity of your desire to repeat the action.**

What does the prize look like?

The prize could be as simple as celebrating when you reach first base after a good plate appearance. It could be as small as a high five walking out of a boardroom after closing a big sale.

Sometimes, the prize is the action itself. It could be the home run, the closed sale, or the special look on your spouse's face across the table when you're out to dinner on a date night.

Maybe it's quietly relaxing with a glass of wine at the end of a good day when you accomplished a lot of things that were important to you.

When you reframe your trigger and change your actions, your brain responds favorably because you've achieved greater alignment. **Instead of battling your brain, your brain rewards you.**

You may be asking yourself, is a prize important? Absolutely!

When you give yourself a prize, **you create an essential reinforcement for the trigger and the action**. You lock in the habit through the chemical reaction you create in your brain.

Changing enough habits and getting more prizes is part of a larger overall enhanced state of being. Each time you put One More new habit in place, you'll be happier because you're more productive in advancing your life the way you were meant to do.

At the beginning of this chapter, I told you that these steps would be simple, and they are. Don't overthink how you go about developing One More Habit.

1. **Create a new trigger.**
2. **Execute a new action.**
3. **Enjoy the prize.**

Because of the way your brain is hard-wired, you're going to constantly engage in your habits. When you create the right habits, you'll save energy and time. Neuroplasticity means that you can accomplish this hard-wiring and create new habits in as little as 30 days the vast majority of the time.

Examine your current emotions and intentionally look for ways you can create new habits. Also, intentionally look for ways to eliminate habits that don't serve you well.

When you look for One More opportunities to create new habits, you'll find a clear path to a more blissful life.

Perhaps most important of all, **One More Habit could not only change your life, that habit could also save your life**.

Eating healthy, exercising regularly, getting plenty of sleep, enjoying your hobbies, volunteering in your community, and other similar habits are things that you should actively pursue.

I started this chapter by saying "show me your habits and I'll show you your life." I hope that statement makes more sense for you now.

Our habits have consequences. If we take control of our habits on a more consistent basis, we'll have a higher measure of control over the results we achieve. That's why it's essential as a One More thinker to understand the science of habits and the need to be intentional with our actions to positively alter the outcomes in our lives.

13

One More Multiplier

The whole is greater than the sum of its parts.
—A guiding principle of Gestalt psychology

HOW OFTEN DO YOU COME IN CONTACT WITH FORCES THAT TRANSCEND THE TASKS AT HAND? Forces that create results exceeding expectations. **You may sense you're a part of something special, even if you can't put your finger on it.** For some reason, the average transforms into something magical.

Often, it only takes adding one small thing for this to happen. It can be subtle. Or it can be obvious, producing a seismic shift that triggers a tsunami multiplier effect.

The Dynamics of Team Chemistry

Change is natural. At times, you'll seek change. At other times, change will find you. **Don't fear change.** When you accept your new reality, the most amazing things can happen. In a lab experiment, there are control elements that don't change, and there are variables introduced to create different sets of results.

The same holds true for your interactions with others. **Some parts of your life will have constants in it, and other parts will change, leading you in new directions.** Whether you're talking about business, sports, families, or other types of relationships, this is the case. Adding or taking away variables and people changes the team chemistry of whatever you're involved with.

Great team chemistry produces a multiplier effect. Bad team chemistry will burn your efforts down to the ground. Good team chemistry requires having the right pieces in the right places.

There are few better examples than the 1980 U.S. Men's Olympic hockey team. Dubbed the "Miracle on Ice," coach Herb Brooks created a new definition for team chemistry by assembling a roster that went on to beat the heavily favored Russians, and ultimately won the gold medal.

The win was improbable, to say the least. "I'm not looking for the best players. I am looking for the right players," was one of the more memorable lines uttered by Kurt Russell, who played Brooks in the movie *Miracle* that followed a few years later.

Everybody loves playing with a superstar on their team, but if that high level of talent also brings disruption and upsets team chemistry, then you should think long and hard about whether or not to add that piece to your team in the first place.

Good team chemistry requires trust, respect, and loyalty to each other and your team while also pursuing your individual goals. Good team chemistry is all about **dividing and conquering tasks and multiplying your victory celebrations.** Cooperation and sacrificing the self for the good of the whole mean **setting aside your ego for a bigger purpose.** There is strength in numbers and a common purpose.

Ecclesiastes 4:12 tells us, *"And if one prevails against him, two shall withstand him; and a threestrand cord is not quickly broken."* Understanding team and individual weaknesses and then showing up to work on those weaknesses daily are also critical. **Commitment to long-term success is essential. Talent alone will not carry the day.**

However, when talent combines with these other factors, the resulting good team chemistry creates a One More multiplier effect to produce over-the-top results.

Greatness Attracts Greatness

Let's keep things simple. When a One More multiplier is in play . . .

$$1 + 1 = 3$$

In your business or your personal relationships, when you attract the right person who complements and elevates your natural state, the sum of that partnership is greater than the sum of the individual parts. High achievers and fully functioning human beings understand this, and that's why they seek out like-minded people. **Greatness *can* exist on its own. It often does. But smart people know the absolute best results don't happen when greatness exists in a one-person vacuum.**

An optimal state happens when you challenge greatness. It could be an opposing force or a force that aligns with a singular greater purpose. **The entire foundation of marriage is built on alignment. Two become one, but that "one" is a union that transcends the two people before they joined in matrimony.**

How many times have you heard this: "He makes the players around him better"? Those who are One More multipliers seek out worthy challenges and people who will propel them to the next level. Michael Jordan was a stud on his own. But when he joined forces with Scottie Pippen, they formed the core of a basketball juggernaut.

You know about Steve Jobs's accomplishments at Apple. You could argue he was destined for greatness anyway, but you can't diminish the counterbalance of partnering with Steve Wozniak. Together, they revolutionized personal computing and built one of the most successful companies ever.

Sometimes, a One More multiplier reveals itself in a different way. Many people believe the "one more piece" in the Chicago Bulls dynasty years was coach Phil Jackson. The same can be said for Pat Riley as he led the Los Angeles Lakers to four titles during the Showtime era.

Don't underestimate a One More multiplier's ability to be an effective recruiter, too. High-level talent wants to work with and be challenged by other high-level talent. **They enjoy the competitiveness and camaraderie of being around their equals.** They also understand how outsized results are possible when high-level forces combine to create a unified vision.

His Name Is Thomas Edward Patrick Brady, Jr.

You know him better as Tom Brady.

Thousands of pages have already been written about him, and there's not much I can add to his legendary successes. What I can do is show you how even Tom Brady can go from a centerpiece on one team to a One More multiplier on another team.

In 2020, Tom Brady became the One More multiplier for the Tampa Bay Buccaneers. With Brady at the helm, the team went from a losing season the year before to winning a Super Bowl in 2021. **You may have a hard timing thinking of Tom Brady as the One More piece to anything.** He was the essence of the New England Patriots dynasty for 20 seasons, racking up 16 division titles and 6 Super Bowl wins.

Still, in football, as it is in life, everything has an expiration date. Most guys would hang up the cleats after a run like that. But most guys are not Tom Brady. Against the backdrop of the Covid-19 pandemic, when America was desperate for heroes, Tom Brady became a One More Cinderella story. He ensured his place in football history as the greatest player of all time.

Brady and the Tampa Bay Buccaneers raised more than a few eyebrows when the team signed him to a two-year, $50 million deal. The team had finished 2019 with a disappointing 7-9 record. Management felt they had an excellent foundation to build on, so signing Brady was a calculated risk that created immediacy to their efforts. As it turns out, they got a bargain.

Brady brought a warrior mentality that elevated teammates to play some of the best football of their entire careers. Their will to win completely changed with Brady added to the mix. Brady became the ultimate One More multiplier.

As he has done throughout his career, **Brady also made it clear about what he expected out of his teammates.** He's been consistent in his belief that "You can't go out and practice average on Wednesday, average on Thursday, okay on Friday, and then expect to play well on Sunday." The stage was set. As multipliers often do, he recruited a ton of talented skill players who wanted to play on a Tom Brady team.

Lock in on this: One More multipliers attract One More multipliers.

Shortly after signing Brady, the Bucs added Leonard Fournette at running back. They traded with the Patriots for Rob Gronkowski. And they signed Antonio Brown as a free agent late in the season. In the process, the team turned things around and finished 11-5 in the regular season.

"To me, football is so much about mental toughness. It's digging deep, doing whatever you need to do to help a team win, and that comes in a lot of shapes and forms," said Brady earlier in his career. And that's exactly what he did in the 2020 season.

It may not be the first thing that comes to mind, but one of the ways to do whatever it takes is the ability of a One More multiplier to attract highly skilled talent, which is critical when building a championship team. Why was that so important in this case? Because other than a Ryan Succop field goal, Brady and those One Mores were responsible for every score in the Bucs 31-9 Super Bowl win.

Here's how stunning Brady's accomplishment was. He became the first pro athlete in any of the four major American sports to win a championship with two different teams after turning 40. He also became the first player in NFL history to defeat three former Super Bowl MVPs in the same postseason, beating the Saints' Drew Brees, the Packers' Aaron Rodgers, and the Chiefs' Patrick Mahomes. Brady bested them all!

Tom Brady sets the standard as a One More multiplier by bringing equanimity and an unmatched work ethic, smarts, and an uncompromising expectation of others. He's been quoted thousands of times throughout his career. For my money, the one quote that sums up who Tom Brady is and what he brings to his team is what he said when someone once asked him which Super Bowl ring was his favorite.

Tom simply replied, *"The next one."*

Adding the Right Kind of One More Multiplier

While undeniably talented, it would be a complete waste to have two Peyton Mannings on one team. Manning needed equally gifted wide receivers to catch his passes. Without skilled receivers like Marvin Harrison, Manning's accomplishments would still be considerable. But would they be legendary?

For his part, Harrison didn't do too bad playing with Manning. The eight-time Pro Bowler finished his career with more than 14,000 receiving yards. His 1,102 receptions are second only to Jerry Rice for the most all-time. Of those, 971 were catches from Manning. Together, they own every major quarterback-to-receiver record. That includes the most touchdowns, completions, and yards.

Adding the right kind of One More piece creates a multiplier effect. That synergy usually defies description. Two people, or a team of several people, in sync with their standards and goals, often rise and defeat more talented teams that don't possess the same dynamics.

Working with One More Multipliers

The One More piece to a puzzle in business, sports, or any team endeavor changes the energy level, interactions, and results at all levels. **There is a trickle-down effect when people buy into the leadership a One More multiplier brings to a team.** If you manage that team and add a One More multiplier, you'll have greater success if you follow a few rules related to your multiplier:

- **Educate them on the bigger picture.** One Mores respect clarity and can often contribute to areas outside of their primary responsibilities. Doing so also makes them better team players by default instead of only being interested in personal ego-driven accomplishments.
- **Give them a voice to contribute.** Multipliers are natural leaders, even if they are normally internalized and quiet as a rule. Their accomplishments draw others to them. Says Tom Peters, *"Leaders don't create followers. They create more leaders."* When many pieces of the team take on leadership responsibilities, it lightens the load for everyone. Teammates also respect One More multipliers. They'll listen to a multiplier's input and trust their track record will produce continued positive outcomes.
- **Create a framework of autonomy.** Your One More will remain more engaged and productive when they're allowed to make decisions independently when possible. Don't micromanage them. Delegate when possible. If the opportunity presents itself, consider asking your star to mentor others to develop both the star and the mentee.
- **Remove obstacles and let them be the stars at what they do best.** Do you have a super salesman who spends too

much time tracking down paperwork and submitting mindless reports? Would you put your IT rock star on a Human Resources policy committee? Do accountants make good marketers as a rule? Strategically place your One More multipliers in the places where they'll be the happiest and most productive. *And then leave them alone.*

- **Challenge them to compete at a high level.** That doesn't always come from teammates. Often, a coach will challenge a One More player to compete against themselves. If your batting average was .300 last year, what will it take to hit .325 this year? If you made $2 million in sales last year, how can you get to $2.5 million this year? One More multipliers thrive on competition. Give them the tools they need and watch them go to work.
- **As a leader, you need to be sure you check your ego at the door.** You must put the team's needs first and strategize how a multiplier can most effectively contribute and impact an overall effort.
- **Be sure to listen for feedback.** Recognize the difference between excuses and legitimate issues holding back your One More multiplier and your entire team.
- Most of all, **learn to let go at the right time and when to lead at the right time.** Use time-outs, emails and memos, sales meetings, "we have to talk" discussions, and other communication efforts sparingly for maximum effect.

Joining forces with a One More multiplier is a challenging and exciting proposition. You don't get to sit back and be passive once you do. Multipliers won't tolerate it.

Bring your best game. You'll need it. And I guarantee the effort will be worth it.

14

~ ✕ ~

One More
Inconvenience

*The ultimate measure of a man is not where he stands in
moments of comfort and convenience, but where he stands at
times of challenge and controversy.*

—*Dr. Martin Luther King, Jr.*

HERE'S A SIMPLE BUT COMPELLING FACT
ABOUT THE WAY THE WORLD WORKS.

Convenience and greatness cannot co-exist. They are
diametrically opposed forces. If you can accept that many of the
great things you want in life will be inconvenient from start to
finish, you're well on your way to becoming a One More thinker.

Inconveniences are the challenges you must overcome to have a shot at accomplishing anything significant. These inconveniences can be anything from getting up at 5 a.m. to make a 7 a.m. meeting with your professor when you're working on your Masters' degree, or running 75 miles a week to prep for your first marathon, even though your feet are on fire because they're covered with blisters. It could be going through four months of morning sickness before you give birth. Or putting in 60 hours a week to be the top salesperson for your company.

Paying the price of inconvenience is no guarantee you'll succeed. But if you don't inconvenience yourself and confront the difficult things in front of you, you'll have no chance at ending up where you want to be in life.

Embracing Inconvenience as a Way of Life

Think about the most extraordinary things you've been blessed with in your life. Chances are, they started as something inconvenient. A championship you won. Adding 25 pounds of muscle while lowering your body fat by 50 percent. Earning a raise or a promotion at work. You sacrificed some parts of your life to reach these goals. Even if you did so willingly, those sacrifices came with some degree of inconvenience attached to them.

However, on the other side of all these amazing accomplishments are the most exceptional memories, events, relationships, and possessions in your life. That's why, as unusual at it may seem, **if you want a fulfilling and blissful existence, you must embrace inconvenience as a way of life**.

Let me pose this question to you: If you have a daily or weekly "To Do" list, how do you attack that list?

Often, to make ourselves feel like we're accomplishing something, we'll do the easy things first. That's because doing the easy stuff is usually recommended and, in some cases, celebrated. Celebrate if you want. But all you're doing is celebrating being average and ordinary.

What if you started attacking your day by doing the most difficult and inconvenient things? Not "first things first" or "feared things first." **Start by doing difficult and inconvenient things first.** Doing hard things builds character. It separates you from the pack. When you do hard, challenging, and inconvenient things, you'll soon realize your biggest, best, and most amazing dreams are on the other side of the tallest hills you must climb.

It's not the correct mindset to put pressure on yourself to do inconvenient things either. You also need to enjoy doing them. I guarantee you will be a much happier person in the end. **Satisfaction and self-esteem come from accomplishing inconvenient tasks.**

But instead of embracing the inconvenient, most of us avoid it. The unfortunate byproduct is that we never fully realize what we're capable of and who the best version of ourselves is.

The Relationship Between Inconvenience and Controversy

When you decide to do something great with your life, get ready. **You're going to be controversial. Controversy is inconvenient. Inconvenience ruffles feathers.**

Going with the flow, kicking back, and chilling means you'll never take any heat. You'll never be uncomfortable. You'll never be inconvenienced. But you'll also never do anything great either.

If you're a leader of any sort, whether a CEO, a captain of a team, or even a leader of your family, you must **challenge those under you to do uncomfortable and inconvenient things as well**. It's the only way they'll achieve greatness too. As a leader, it's part of what you're charged with doing.

Great leaders are often great mentors. You mentor people by getting them to become One More thinkers and do inconvenient things that will create personal and professional growth. You must create a culture in your company, your team, or your own family of doing unknown, demanding, and inconvenient things. If you're diligent in this area, the collective results will be stunning.

Now take those short-term accomplishments and apply the variable of time. **Think about the possibilities when you stack up one month, one year, or a decade's worth of doing inconvenient things.** When you can build the habit of doing inconvenient things into your life over time, can you imagine how amazing your life will be?

The Relationship Between Inconvenience and Greatness

Your biggest dreams never materialize if you gravitate toward convenience. Convenience and your optimum health do not co-exist. Your ideal relationship is never born out of convenience. If you want to be wealthy, the path to a bigger bank account will be incredibly challenging and by no means convenient. **When you live a life of convenience, you are at**

odds with living a life of greatness. If anything has come to you in a particularly easy way, you may like the result, but you will not savor it as much as something else you had to struggle and fight to achieve.

Our minds are not only hard-wired solely to seek comfort and convenience. For many of us, we're also hard-wired to ease up on the gas when we think we've gotten to where we want to be with some part of our life. We often tell ourselves we want only the best outcomes, and we may even try to design a life that appears to point to a higher level. But in reality, **we often create processes to avoid inconvenience and conflict. When we do this, we're steering ourselves toward a life that already exists.**

To further justify our efforts, we even enlist others to confirm we're on the right path. Those people often collude with us in our self-deception. Don't beat yourself up if this sounds like you. It happens to a lot of people more often than not. We also compare ourselves to others instead of drawing on our own values and capabilities. **Mimicking others is an act of convenience.** When we become leaders of our own lives, we don't copy anyone. We recognize our journey is ours alone. It's okay to draw on others as sources of inspiration and knowledge. In fact, it's essential.

However, you must be mindful enough to know where to draw the line. You must figure out how to cherry-pick the right information and use it to your fullest advantage. That's not to say you shouldn't make your life more convenient. But you must understand the role convenience plays in achieving your highest-level goals and setting your highest-level standards. **It requires fighting your pre-existing habits of working toward** convenience and replacing those with habits centered around results. Those results are the end product of thinking about what you value, applying a standard that aligns with those values, and producing an outcome that thrusts you forward to a more remarkable and authentic life.

Best-selling author Haruki Murakami put it best when he said, "*Your work should be an act of love, not a marriage of convenience.*" If you're only interested in reaching a level of convenience, you'll achieve a lot less than doing whatever it takes when you're committed to a higher level of greatness.

Why You Need Inconvenience in Your Life

If you're going through something challenging, it may be a sign that you're on to something special. It could be unique or even once in a lifetime. **Understand there is a significant difference between inconvenience and problems.**

Robert Fulghum, best-selling author of books like *All I Really Need to Know I Learned in Kindergarten*, explained it this way: "*Life is lumpy. And a lump in the oatmeal, a lump in the throat, and a lump in the breast are not the same lump. One should learn the difference.*"

Learn to recognize the difference between a problem and an inconvenience. Once you do that, here's why you need that inconvenience in your life. Ask any multimillionaire if getting wealthy was convenient. They may enjoy the challenge, but they'll also tell you it was one of the most inconvenient journeys of their lifetime.

If you think it's easy when you're alone at the office while everyone else is out partying on a Friday night . . .

Or you're bleeding money even though you're working your butt off to try and sell your dream to anybody who will listen . . .

Or you're weary from the ongoing daunting task of turning over every stone looking for new clients and prospects . . .

. . . then you've never gone through the struggles and challenges it takes to become wealthy like I did for years upon years.

Here's something else we can all relate to: What do you think the response will be if you ask somebody how convenient it was to lose 50, 75, or 100 or more pounds? So many people stay fat for a reason. We all know fat is uncomfortable. But for many people, losing weight is an uncomfortable challenge, despite the obvious benefits. Do you think it's inconvenient to get up and go to the gym on those days when you're sore and your muscles ache because you never worked out that way before? How about prepping all your food in advance, or fighting off cravings for food you love that is also bad for you? Fast-food addictions don't always get the attention they deserve, but many of us stand no chance against the speed, convenience, and taste temptations a Whopper or a Big Mac offers. Even the simple act of drinking a gallon of water a day when you're hooked on sodas is deceptively inconvenient.

The point is this: Inconvenience is a challenge.

Inconvenience is not easy. But in the long run, convenience is a lot worse.

Here's the other thing.

Convenience never lasts. If you don't put in the work, sooner or later, what you've got will go away. It could be flat-out taken away. Your uninspired, lackluster behavior could cause you to drop the ball. **Or fate will simply say "enough," and the**

powers of the universe will put you in a different set of circumstances. **Rarely are those circumstances better.**

One More thinkers do hard and inconvenient things because they understand what it means when they do them. **They attack inconvenient things with a sense of urgency.** Life becomes more meaningful when you realize after you live a moment, it's gone forever. You can never get it back. And **wasted time is one of the biggest crimes you can commit against yourself.**

Seek Inconvenient Relationships

You can't navigate this world alone. What do you look for in a relationship? Is it trust? Respect? Empathy? Honesty? Good relationships are built on many foundational pillars. But I'll bet you never thought one of those pillars is inconvenience. The fact is that **friendships and loving relationships built on convenience are not quality relationships.** The best relationships are not about being by your side only when it's convenient. It's about being there when it's not.

When you're in trouble . . .

When you need help . . .

Those close to you will rally around you and be willing to sacrifice some part of their being, even if it's inconvenient for them. You might need money. Or a shoulder to cry on. Maybe your car broke down, and you need a ride to and from work for a week. It could be something as simple and just being a good listener. **Recognize the difference between someone who takes time to talk with you when they have free time versus someone who frees up their time to talk to you.**

See the difference?

Over time, relationships of convenience reveal themselves in many ways. **But it only takes a single act of revealing ourselves during times of inconvenience that matters the most.** Good friends and lovers tell inconvenient truths, not to hurt you, but to help you. Instead of getting angry, be grateful. **Treat truth like gold, even when you are stung by it.**

Enduring a sacrifice when something doesn't directly impact you is inconvenient. It is also the hallmark of the type of people you want in your life. Sacrifice goes beyond convenience. Responding to another person's inconvenience builds bridges that can last a lifetime. **The same applies to your relationship with your God. Faith built on convenience is nothing more than a hollow faith.** You will never enjoy a close and spiritual relationship with your God until you ask for help when it's not convenient. Seek relationships that can withstand the rigors of life and the inconveniences that both sides will need help with over time.

You want convenience? That's best left to a visit to a fast-food restaurant for a quarter pounder with cheese. You want people in your life who are glad and willing to accept the consequences of inconvenience. **It is a direct reflection of their character and their level of respect for you.**

Tapping into the Right Kind of Inconvenience

Ask yourself these questions.

- What kind of life do I want to lead?
- Who are the people I want in my life?
- What are my standards for reaching the goals I have?

Will you get the answers you want by living a convenient life? I'll save you the trouble of having to think about it. The answer is a big, fat . . .

NO!

When you have these answers, you'll be well on your way to understanding how much and what kind of inconvenience you'll tolerate in your life. How will you know if these answers are your truth or not?

Simple.

The best and most productive people in the world pursue inconvenient things and handle them with a temperament of equanimity. Equanimity is the key. When you can achieve mental calmness, composure, and control, especially in a difficult situation, you will know you have tapped into the right kind of inconvenience.

Inconvenience is a direct corollary to the amount of commitment you have. As legendary motivator Ken Blanchard explains it, *"There is a difference between interest and commitment. When you're interested in doing something, you only do it when it's convenient. When you're committed to something, you accept no excuses, only results."*

When you accept only results, you are practicing a form of equanimity. Because you will only accept one outcome, distractions and a lesser level of performance are stripped away. You are calm and composed because your path is clear.

Equanimity is essential when you're doing inconvenient things. Without it, you'll eventually burn out. **You can't sustain inconvenient efforts and rise to another level unless you approach life with the right mental mindset.** Although equanimity is essential, it can be too much of a good thing as well.

Some people are really calm. Too calm. They have a ton of equanimity in their lives. But they never try anything difficult. That creates a false sense of equanimity. To be successful, you must combine inconvenience and equanimity. Equanimity is a form of emotional control rooted in your thoughts. Inconvenient deeds are based in your actions.

It's not easy. I've struggled with this over the years. I've been pretty good about doing difficult things but not always with the requisite equanimity. I've succeeded but with more chaos and stress than was necessary. I'm not alone. Many mega-achievers do inconvenient things every day. But they're not happy.

To those people, I say this: **If you can't enjoy the beautiful bounties bestowed upon you with equanimity, you're not living your best life.**

Inconvenience is essential, but you must make sure you practice it the right way to achieve the best possible results in your life.

15

One More and Defining Leadership

If you want to lift yourself up, lift up someone else.
—Booker T. Washington

THE CONCEPT OF LEADERSHIP IS AS OLD AS CIVILIZATION ITSELF, and I doubt there's a personal development topic that's been studied or written about more.

So, what does it mean to be a One More leader?

As I define it, you are a One More leader if you help people do things they would not otherwise accomplish without your presence. If you can't do that as a leader, there's no need for you.

Whether you realize it or not, **you're already a leader**. At a minimum, you lead yourself. You may also lead your family, employees, teammates, when you practice your religious doctrine, and several other ways.

For our purpose, the question then becomes, "How can I use the concept of One More to become better at leading others?"

There are those who make the case that people are born leaders. That may be so, but I also firmly believe that **leadership is a learned trait**. Everyone has it within themselves to be an effective leader if they decide to work at it.

To do this, start by taking a closer look at what the elements of leadership are.

The Elements of Leadership

I've had the honor of being a leader in my family, on sports teams, for multiple businesses, and in several other capacities in my life.

What I'm about to share are universal leadership elements that transcend who you are or where you're at in your life, whether you're an athlete, a coach, a parent, or a business leader. These elements include:

- selling a big dream;
- everyone is born with unique gifts;
- six basic needs drive us.

Selling a Big Dream

As a leader, it's critical for you to sell a big dream. Let me illustrate this powerful point.

You need to sell a big enough dream so that the dreams of everyone you lead can fit inside the one you're selling.

For example, if you're Clemson football coach Dabo Sweeney, you might sell the idea that not only does everyone fit inside the dream; the dream could also be historic—one that will be remembered for the ages. This could mean going undefeated, having a record number of players drafted into the NFL, or setting other performance marks that have never been achieved before.

Giving people a sense they are involved in something historic is a key step in how you build a culture. That culture means that each individual player and everyone connected to the team is involved in a bigger dream.

A dream much bigger than they can imagine on their own.

Another critical element is that when you work with the people you lead, **help them understand that by making history, they are also making a difference in their lives and many other lives as well.**

Think bigger.

Dare to challenge yourself to make history.

Talk bigger.

Sell others on the idea that the big dream makes a difference.

Act bigger.

Do the hard work involved with selling the dream and let your people see you doing it.

Are you catching this?

Leadership is about executing small things very well but thinking and talking about big things repetitiously. **Your number**

one priority is to sell a big dream, and probably bigger than the one you're thinking about now. It must be all-encompassing!

As a parent, you must sell a big enough dream so that your spouse and your children can see themselves fitting inside the dream you're selling.

If you lead a church, your dream must be big enough so that all the members of the congregation can fit their dreams and aspirations inside of it.

As a business leader, the dream must be big enough so that every employee can also see themselves inside of that dream. If you run a large manufacturing company, you need to sell a big enough dream so you can meet the needs of your customers because you can satisfy the dreams of everyone you lead in that company.

There are too few leaders in the world today who sell a big enough dream. You show me any great leader, and I'll show you a leader who is selling a big dream that captures the hearts, desires, and emotions of everyone they lead.

The dream you're selling as a family leader or a business leader should encompass your values and your vision. A dream is what you stand for, your vision of the future, and the difference you're going to make in the world.

Why is this so important?

As a leader, you're in a different place than everyone else. As a leader, by definition, you're out in front. You have a different viewpoint and perspective than the people standing behind you. Your job is to tell those people what you see.

Tell those people how amazing it's going to be and keep telling them over and over again. It's your obligation as a leader by position alone to effectively do this. From their position, they can't see it as you can. So, you must get them to see it from your position.

Here's another critical point:

Everybody you lead does not have to believe what you're saying!

Isn't that crazy?

They only need to believe that YOU believe what you're saying.

Too many leaders constantly try to get people to believe what they are saying. That comes across as desperate and weak. Great leaders only need to get others to believe that they believe what they're saying.

This is a form of evangelism that I'm going to touch on later.

Everyone Is Born with Unique Gifts

Every person is born with individual talents and geniuses. I call these unique gifts.

Some of these you're born with, and some you develop. As a leader, **if you identify these unique gifts in people, you can lead them in a way nobody else can**. You separate yourself as a leader when you're able to do this.

These gifts can be humor, intellect, resiliency, faith, or kindness. Someone you lead could be blessed with mental toughness, honesty, ambition, creativity, generosity, loyalty, etc. The different kinds of unique gifts are limitless. **This ability to identify these gifts and then link them to the dream you're selling is critical in your effort to lead people under you.**

The other thing I've discovered is that, for the most part, no one has ever pointed these unique gifts out to them. **Typically, people have an innate sense of their unique gifts, but in many cases, they are underutilized because there's been no concerted effort on how to best to apply them.** Most people never meet a real leader in their life, and as a result, they never fulfill their true potential by tapping into these gifts.

To fulfill a person's potential, identify what their gifts are and then apply those gifts to a cause that stirs their hearts. That's your job as a leader.

By validating these unique gifts, what a person has suspected about themselves now becomes their truth. They're filled with more confidence and armed with an understanding of how they fit into an overall game plan. As a result, they'll create more value for the dream and accomplish more than they ever thought possible on their own.

Six Basic Needs Drive Us

Consider the words of my friend Tony Robbins, *"The more you understand what somebody wants, needs, and fears, the more you can figure out how to add value."*

Tony and I are among many who subscribe to the idea that there are six basic human needs. They are:

- Certainty
- Uncertainty and Variety
- Significance
- Love and Connection
- Growth
- Contribution

These are typically discussed in terms of finding your level of happiness. But I want to put them in the context of how you leverage these six basic needs when you lead others. Your goal is to also figure out how to meet these needs for the people you lead.

Ideally, everyone wants all six of these basic needs met all the time. In reality, most people tend to focus on two or three that are the most important to them at a particular time.

Let's look closer at each of these needs.

- **Certainty.** People who want certainty in their lives need to be reassured you can provide them with a stable environment. **They value safety and an ongoing routine.** They fear change and often equate it with some kind of uncomfortable, intimidating process or pain.

  Suppose you're going to lead somebody when their primary basic need is certainty. In that case, you're going to speak to them differently than you would with somebody who places more value on the other basic needs, such as significance.

  Imagine you're able to cast a big dream, identify this person's gifts, and then determine what their most important basic needs are. Can you imagine how productive and happy this person is going to be when they value certainty and that's what you give to them?

- **Uncertainty and Variety.** Those who thrive on uncertainty and variety are **stimulated by the unknown and change**. They fear getting stuck in a rut or doing the same thing every day. They want new, exciting, and different tasks as often as possible.

  When leading these people, you need to promote the dream, identify these people's gifts, and then put them in positions that give them the type of variety they want.

- **Significance.** When people seek significance, **they want to know their efforts are valued and important.** They want recognition, and often this is more important to them than money. They enjoy the spotlight and they'll work hard if they know a high-profile reward is attached to their efforts.

   If you're going to lead people who are significance-driven, you need to **flood them with recognition at every possible opportunity.**

   For example, if you coach a team, it's on you to create a culture that promotes significance for the players. If you're a parent, it's incumbent on you to make sure you praise your children who value significance and recognition. Suppose you're a business leader, and you have people in your organization who are competitive and results-driven. In that case, it's up to you to create a framework that links those people's gifts with their primary needs for recognition.

- **Love and Connection.** Love is the strongest of all emotions. **There is a universal need among everyone to feel a connection and closeness to another person or cause.** The greatest poetry and music ever created are about love. Wars have been fought for the love of country. And if you ever doubt the power and universality of love, look no further than to a mother's or a father's love for their children.

   People who are driven by love and connection want to belong to a cause bigger than they are. Whether you're in business, coaching a team, or in any other situation where you're leading a group of people with many love-driven members, you need to communicate that they are part of a family.

   You need to make these people feel they are accepted, cared for, and loved. Let these people know this often.

Imagine leading one or more people who are driven by love and dropping messages of significance or variety on them. Those may be great messages, but you're applying them to the wrong people.

Also, **don't make messages about your needs**. This applies in all cases, but as an example, even if you value things, such as certainty or significance, you should not be sending out those kinds of messages if the people you lead value love strongly.

As a leader, your messages need to be targeted to the people you lead.

- **Growth.** Others place a high value on growing their minds, skills, and experiences. You need to meet this need by **placing challenges in front of these people and giving them the sense they're growing as part of your organization.** This energizes them. They get excited when you ask them to solve problems of increasing magnitude and complexity.

  If you're a coach, you need to let your players know they're improving their skills. As a business leader, when you're leading someone who values growth, you need to let them know they're growing due to all the hard work they're putting in related to the dream and vision you created for them.

- **Contribution.** Others are driven by the need to contribute. Some people feel they're at their best when they help others through their service or expertise to support a cause or a goal. These people are not driven by significance or recognition. They may not care one way or another about certainty or uncertainty.

  To feel valued and fulfilled, **they need to know they are contributing and making a difference.** You need to message these kinds of things regularly.

Basic Needs Can Change Over Time

As a great leader, also understand that each person's needs can change over time. When I was younger, to get the most out of me, you needed to link competition, recognition, and growth to what I needed to do.

Throughout my adult life, I've been fulfilled by a lot of significance and recognition. I've also been blessed with a lot of certainty, variety, and love. However, over time, my needs have evolved. And now, if you're leading me, you need to connect with me with the primary need of contribution.

That wasn't the case 15 years ago. If you wanted to convince me to come and speak to your group, do you know how you would sell me on doing it? You would have to tell me there were going to be thousands of people who were going to love me, cheer, clap, jump up and down, and tell me what an amazing job I did when I was done because I was very significance and recognition oriented.

Now, if you use those reasons as of way to try and convince me to come and speak to your group, that wouldn't stimulate me, and I will probably turn you down. But if you contact me and tell me that if I speak to your group that it would make a huge difference to those people's lives, change the direction of your company, and make a huge contribution, then you will hook me.

Do you see the difference of how a different message at a different time would get me to act?

My primary basic need now is contribution. **It's the reason I'm writing this book.**

I'm not writing this book so millions of people will acknowledge my work, although that would be nice. **I'm writing this book because I think it will help change millions of people's lives. I want to help people by helping them meet their most important basic needs. By doing so, I'm meeting my own most important basic need as well.**

To become a great leader, you must look less at who you are and more at the people you're leading. They're the ones you're asking to produce results on your mission's behalf. **When they're effective because their needs are met, your needs are met by default.** And everyone in the group benefits.

This is true whether you're a parent, a coach of a sports team, a small business owner, or the CEO of a Fortune 500 company.

Validate Your Leadership by Setting an Example

I want you to remember this . . . **most things in life are caught, not taught.**

Most people will learn a lot more in life by watching what you do rather than by what they do when you simply try to teach them.

Holding yourself to a higher standard is essential when you lead other people.

If what you ask other people to do isn't consistent with what you ask of yourself, the people you lead will quickly recognize this, and you have undermined your own efforts.

Your leadership example starts by consistently reinforcing the big dream and making sure everyone knows they're a part of that dream. Also, take time to figure out what each person's unique gifts are and demonstrate a willingness to make sure other people's basic needs are met.

More specifically, **always do One More**. Show up one hour earlier than everyone else in the office. Make One More business contact than everybody else. Put in One More level of preparation for presentations and meetings.

Remember: all eyes are on you.

Setting a poor example dooms you and your dream to failure. If you're having trouble becoming an effective leader, the first place you should look for improvement is at yourself. **You can't ask others to perform at a high level if you can't first ask it of yourself.**

Now that we've defined what leadership is, let's take a look at how we can put these elements into action.

16

One More and My 11 Leadership Principles

The test of an organization is not genius. It is its capacity to make common people achieve uncommon performance.

—Peter F. Drucker

I'VE DEFINED THE ELEMENTS OF LEADERSHIP AND WHAT IT TAKES TO BE A ONE MORE LEADER. To put those elements into practice, I follow several key leadership principles. By practicing these principles, I've produced significant results for myself over the years. You may benefit by incorporating them into your leadership style as well.

Keep in mind, because **leadership is a lifelong learning process**, this list is dynamic. As I continue to grow, I add and subtract to this list from time to time.

Here are the 11 leadership principles I currently practice.

1. Become an Evangelist

According to the Merriam-Webster dictionary, one of the definitions of an "evangelist" is someone who talks about something with great enthusiasm.

The best leaders enroll others in their cause. They are evangelists for their dreams.

Much like a shepherd guiding a flock, **a great leader is concerned with evangelism in the form of fellowship, discipleship, and service.** I've had the privilege of getting to know Steve Wozniak, one of the founders of Apple. Because I was curious, I asked him what Steve Jobs's gifts were. What was it that made him great? I expected to hear that he was hard-working, resilient, or incredibly intellectually bright.

But that's not what he told me.

He told me **Steve Jobs had an amazing ability to sell the dream,** that he was evangelical about Apple's cause, and that evangelism was infectious throughout the company.

Evangelism is the transference of the dreams you're selling to those you lead so that you can project infectious energy to the rest of the world.

Leading through fellowship strengthens the bond between you, your employees, customers, or family members.

Discipleship means you can effectively pass along your beliefs as a leader to those under you.

Service in leadership is about meeting the basic needs of those under you. This means recognizing your employees for a job well done or loving your family members regularly.

2. Listen and Observe

It's impossible to be a great leader unless you look at the circumstances and people you lead. **This ability to listen and observe helps you identify the gifts and talents of the people around you.**

This can't be done in a void or a haphazard way. You must be intentional and pay focus to even the smallest details. **Never think of absorbing these details as an obligation. Think of it as an investment.**

As a leader, if you can't slow down long enough and take an extra couple of minutes to get into the specifics of the people you lead, then you're leaving a big pile of untapped opportunities and potential sitting on the table. It's one thing to look at a person's resume or see how they conduct themselves in an interview. It's quite another to **look beyond formal measurements to fully understand a person's unique gifts**.

If you're the head coach of a football team, part of what you must do is look at a player's stats to see what they can accomplish on the field. However, you also need to fully understand what kind of a presence they are in the locker room. Are they a positive force who lifts other players up? Do they go all out during every practice? Do they stay late and work hard to improve parts of their game that need more work?

Actions speak volumes about the people you want on your team and how you're going to lead them.

3. Wise Leaders Build Other Leaders

Wise leaders do not hoard leadership opportunities. Instead, they actively look to grow and develop other leaders.

The number one job of a leader is to develop new leaders.

Some leaders are intimidated by developing other leaders around them. They're threatened and prefer to keep power in their own hands. They fail to realize that **when they build leaders, they lighten their load, create loyalty, and make the overall team stronger**.

Think about a parent who teaches their teenager to drive. When that child gets their license, they have taken a huge step forward in personal growth. They now have more freedom, more choices and can help the entire family by running errands to the grocery store or taking younger siblings to practices or games. As a result, the teen is happier, more independent, and confident when taking on more significant challenges. The family dynamic has been reshaped, and parents are now free to reclaim their time to do other productive and enjoyable things.

This is also applicable to businesses. In fact, one of the key job satisfaction metrics often cited by employees is the chance to advance in a company as part of a larger career path. Talented employees often leave for greener pastures when they feel like they've stalled out or aren't given a chance to take a more active role as a leader in a company.

Teams are no different. **You show me any great team, and I'll show you one that is led by great players *and* great coaches.** Think of all the championships that LeBron James or Michael Jordan won as players. Of course, coaches were critical to their success, but it was their player-led leadership that spelled the difference between winning championships or not.

4. Love, Believe In, Care, and Show People How to Live Better

I learned many of the leadership principles I use today from a bunch of 8- to 10-year-old boys.

Shortly after college, I was blessed with the opportunity to work at McKinley Home for Boys as a youth counselor. Little did I know that when I first walked into Cottage 8 my entire world would change.

At that time, McKinley was a group home for orphaned or molested boys, with parents who were incarcerated, or had no other adult who could take care of them for various reasons. From my first day, I found myself in a position where **all those boys wanted from me was to love them, believe in them, care about them, and show them how to live better**. And frankly, I didn't feel qualified to do it at the time.

Just like me, **many of you probably don't feel qualified right now to be a leader**. When you feel this way, draw upon this thought I often reference, "God doesn't call the qualified, He qualifies the called." At McKinley, I didn't feel qualified, but I did understand that I was called to be there.

Since that time, one of the secrets to life I've learned is that every person of every age wants the same things as those boys. If you're a senior executive, when a 35-year-old executive walks into your office, the main thing he or she wants from you as a leader is to love, care, believe, and show him or her how to live better.

If you're going to be a great leader, your success is directly connected to these things. When you can incorporate them, you'll get people to do what they otherwise would not do without your presence.

So often, we miss opportunities to make a difference this way. My time at McKinley taught me **you can make a difference as a leader, anytime and anywhere.** Even the smallest acts of encouragement and kindness can make a huge difference in the lives of people around you.

This is the ultimate definition of leadership.

5. Repetition, Repetition, Repetition

Leadership is not about saying new things to old people, it's about saying old things to new people.

Too often, as a leader, we try too hard to come up with new things to say to our team. The fact is that **great leaders are willing to repeat themselves over and over again.** I call this **"suffering from leadership fatigue"** because you get tired of hearing yourself say the same things time and again. But the truth is, you need to overcome this fatigue because it's **your ability to say the same things repeatedly that creates a culture in your organization.**

You must constantly reinforce your messages and sell your dream to others so they fully understand your mission as a leader. This also reinforces the basic need for certainty in many people. **Your messages must be simple** so that everyone can clearly understand them. Treat these messages and the number of times you repeat them like a crusade.

All successful entrepreneurs are this way. When you meet them, you know exactly what they're about. Their reputation precedes them. This is the way they build a successful brand. **They create pre-existing positive ideas about who they are** and what they stand for through ongoing repetition that's memorable and easy to understand.

In all cases, whatever outlets you use should be consistent in this repetition. As a businessperson, your marketing, social media, sales materials, emails, and every other piece of outreach should reinforce your mission. If you want to undermine your efforts, put out confusing and conflicting messages and see how successful you are.

Effective parenting also requires repetition. You must constantly express your values, beliefs, and expectations to your children. Don't assume you can say something once and a child will take it in and remember it.

As a leader, **get to a place where every person you lead can infectiously repeat your message back to you.** That makes the people you lead your most significant assets in pursuit of your dreams.

6. Be Generous with Recognition

Constantly look for ways to recognize people.

If you're going to build a great organization, it needs to be predicated on competition and recognizing achievements. **All great organizations are competitive. They foster that mindset and acknowledge accomplishments. Recognition is critical.**

Recognizing people for being One More thinkers and doers is a great form of leadership. Conversely, if you're not creating an environment where competition and recognition are important, you miss out on maximizing potential in business, family, or sports.

Effective leaders are great at acknowledging and recognizing people. This leadership principle is so easy to implement, but it's also overlooked way too often. That shouldn't be the case. **Remember, as a basic human need, people thrive on recognition to feel significant.**

I've discovered that while people often equate recognition with significance, what they really want is love. After all, in many people's minds, **recognition is a form of love.**

Remember when we were kids, and our parents recognized our efforts when we brought home an A on a test or hit a home run in a ballgame? Our need for recognition was a way for us to hope our parents would acknowledge they loved us even more.

As adults, we never lose this basic human need. It's hard-wired into our DNA. That's why everyone you meet wants to be loved, cared for, believed in, and have you show them how to do better.

As a leader, people look up to you. What you say matters. **Your words are oversized, and what may seem like a small, offhand comment to you can mean all the difference in the world to people under you.**

Always find a way to be encouraging. **Find ways to praise people publicly and privately.** There's something incredibly powerful about lifting up a person in front of their peers. There's also an incredible but different kind of power that comes from recognizing someone with a one-on-one personal and sincere thank-you.

As a leader, also **be creative with your recognition**. Not all of it needs to be based on pure performance. Some of that recognition can be based on executing core principles. You can also acknowledge people who do the small things, like showing up early or showing up to work every day over the course of a year.

Awards, plaques, and all manners of verbal or written acknowledgments are highly effective ways of recognizing someone. I like to write personal letters to the children of the mothers and fathers of people who work for me, letting them know how amazing their parents are. This is a form of recognition that almost nobody utilizes.

I'm constantly trying to find unique and innovative ways to recognize the people I lead. It's important to create this kind of culture. Remember, one of the six basic needs is significance (see Chapter 15), and a key element of that is recognition. Another basic need is love, and when you give people recognition, it extends a form of love to them.

7. Have a Cause, Crusade, and a Mission

Show me any great organization, and I'll show you one that is cause- and mission-driven. These places are single-minded and ferociously focused on their end game.

As a leader, when you create a mission and convince people to buy into it, this is another form of meeting a basic human need. In this case, that need is contribution. It's also a huge element of being evangelical when people are asked to rally around a cause bigger than themselves.

A mission has two components:

1. **What are we for?** You must define what you believe in and then inspire people to rally around this crusade. What is our mission statement and our core values? What are the

elements we believe in and how do they contribute to us creating a great place to be?

2. **What are we against?** A mission has to have an enemy. There needs to be something you're against. For example, if you lead a food bank, then you're against hunger. If you own a gym, your enemy could be obesity.

Think of it like being part of a sports rivalry like the Red Sox and Yankees or the Lakers and the Celtics. Obviously, if you're for one team, then it's a safe bet you're against the other. It's one thing to win a championship, but that goes to the next level when you're playing against your rival.

The best enemies are usually something you're trying to eradicate or change. As a director of a women's shelter, you're working to end domestic abuse. If you own a wealth management company, you could be trying to change how people invest money or eliminate bad financial decisions.

The stronger or more emotionally driven you make both components, the easier it is to lead those who buy into them.

Also, like a leader for any great crusade, you must make it a point to **stand in front of your troops and lead them.** You must be willing to take the hits. **Be visible and vocal that you're willing to shield those under you** from criticism or people who want to harm or undermine your efforts.

The perks of leadership fall upon you the most, and so should the burdens as well.

8. Be Authentic and Humble

If you're a liar or a phony, the people you lead may not say it, but they'll know.

When it comes to leadership, **telling the truth is everything**. People will accept that you're not perfect. However, they won't accept when you're not honest. **When you make a mistake, don't try to hide it. Acknowledge it.**

You'd be surprised at how much you endear yourself to people when you simply say, "I made a mistake. I'm sorry, and I'll do better next time."

When you can be truthful about your own performance, you can also be truthful about other people's performance. When you're not authentic about yourself, it's very difficult to create an environment of openness.

Similarly, when people under you make a mistake, if there was no malice attached, **practice compassion** because nobody gets things right all the time.

9. Create a Culture

People are drawn to an overall environment. They want **a culture where a mission, goals, and expectations are clearly defined**.

A well-designed culture takes into account all six of the basic human needs and how to meet them. Culture creates certainty, love, and growth. Recognition and a sense of contribution build morale and a sense of purpose.

Culture is critical because it creates a place where everyone executes their unique geniuses in the present, and everyone also stays focused on the future at the same time. **A healthy culture also values transparency. Questions are embraced, not feared.**

The best companies create cultures because leaders know this allows them to recruit the best employees. **Talented employees**

gravitate to businesses with outstanding cultures because they know tools and resources are in place to help them flourish without negativity or distractions.

10. Give People the Resources They Need to Be Successful

There's nothing worse in life than going into battle with the nagging feeling you don't have enough of what you need to win that battle.

As a leader, it's up to you to properly equip your troops so they feel confident about the challenges you're asking them to tackle. If they must worry about what they don't have, you put them at a distinct disadvantage.

Properly giving your people the resources they need is the battle you must fight before you ask them to do their part on your behalf. This is not a one-time deal. It needs to be part of your culture. It needs to be a constant process.

Resources are not only about training, coaching, supplies, equipment, tools, and an ample budget. You must also work hard at meeting people's basic human needs. When you understand that some employees need certainty, recognition, or growth opportunities, and you take steps to meet those needs, you are giving your people important resources as well.

Also, **ask yourself what resources you need to be an effective leader**. As a CEO, a parent, a coach, or in any other capacity, you need to make sure not to neglect your own resources and basic human needs. You'll undermine your effectiveness when you're not able to operate at peak capacity, too.

11. Build a Movement

Many of you reading this book want to be more than great leaders. You want to build a movement. You want to create massive change on a large scale.

As a reminder, people don't always have to believe what you're saying. **They only have to believe that you believe what you're saying.** However, you need to be persistent, repetitious, and evangelical in your efforts.

Building a movement is a massive and ambitious undertaking. Strong leaders must allow people to see themselves inside the dream, recognize each person's unique gifts, meet people's basic needs, and set an inspirational example to have a chance at a favorable outcome.

Building a movement takes time. But that movement will come toppling down like a house of sticks in a hurricane if you don't start by building a solid foundation and use the best available resources at your disposal.

Being a One More leader is not easy, but when you learn how to apply these leadership principles over time, you not only can propel your life to the highest possible level, you can also elevate the lives of others that you lead as well.

17

One More Degree of Equanimity

Between stimulus and response, there is a space. In that space is
our power to choose our response. In our response lies our
growth and our freedom.
                                      —Victor E. Frankl, neurologist, psychiatrist,
                                                        Holocaust survivor

T O LEAD A BLISSFUL LIFE, YOU MUST SEEK
EQUANIMITY.

In basic terms, equanimity is achieving serenity and mental
calmness in a world filled with stressors. But it's much more
than that. **Equanimity is the quiet glue that underpins a lot of
the other ideas in this book. To reach the highest level of**

these strategies, you must do so with an advanced degree of equanimity.

I am a strong proponent of equanimity. And I think you should be, too.

The Essence of Equanimity

Equanimity originates from the Latin word *æquanimitas* (having an even mind). It is the result of combining *aequus* (even) and *animus* (mind/soul).

Searching for an even mind and soul is an elusive virtue. People spend lifetimes in search of equanimity, me included. I've struggled to find calmness throughout my life. For me, finding equanimity is easier in low-stress situations. However, it's a lot more valuable when I can summon it under duress. **By better understanding what equanimity is and putting it into practice, my paths to success take less time, and are more frequent and substantial.**

Start with this fact.

We can't control the vast majority of what goes on in our lives. We can dream, set standards and goals, and adjust our thinking and actions in a dozen different ways. What we can't do is control outcomes, despite our best efforts. For many people, the natural response is disappointment, frustration, despair, and anger. Nobody is immune from those feelings at one time or another. But what if you could raise your awareness about other ways to condition your brain and your response to outside forces and outcomes? What if you didn't let setbacks negatively impact you? What if you rose above bad outcomes to a positive and rational mental state impervious to those setbacks?

That is the essence of equanimity.

When faced with a difficult situation, such as a stressful phone call, a poor meeting, a financial setback, or a relationship challenge, the highest achievers can find equanimity when others can't. Why do some elite performers rise to an even higher level in crunch time while others wilt? Equanimity is the invisible separator between super-elite performers and those who are average and ordinary.

Think of it this way. A lot of pitchers have an easier time striking out batters in the first inning with nobody on base versus facing a home-run hitter with the bases loaded in the ninth. Golfers can sink putts all round long on a Thursday of a tournament. But how many can use equanimity to sink a 20-footer on the 18th hole on Sunday to win by a stroke? If you're having a rough patch in your relationship, can you use equanimity to say the right thing that will bring the heat down instead of the wrong thing that will have you packing your bags 10 seconds later?

Everyone can find degrees of equanimity most of the time. One of the things that separates them from high achievers is that high achievers can find equanimity when they need it the most.

Equanimity is one of the world's oldest philosophies, and its elements are present in many religions. In Christianity, we often look to each other and say, "Peace be with you" or "The peace of Christ be with you." There are countless examples in the Bible:

The Lord shall fight for you, and ye shall hold your peace.

—Exodus 14:14

Peace I leave with you; My peace I give to you; not as the world gives, do I give to you. Let not your heart be troubled, nor let it be fearful.

—John 14:27

But the meek shall inherit the Earth, and shall delight themselves in the abundance of peace.

—Psalm 37:11

Equanimity is also woven into several eastern Indian religions. For example, Hinduism asks believers to abandon all attachments to success or failure. Elements of Yoga teach that equanimity is attainable through regular meditation and mental disciplines that clear the mind and bring it closer to a healthy balance.

Judaism places importance on equanimity as a necessary foundation for spiritual and moral development.

The Gautama Buddha, a widely followed fifth-century BC philosopher and spiritual teacher, described a mind filled with equanimity as *"abundant, exalted, immeasurable, without hostility and without ill-will."* A few hundred years after his death, he simply became known as Buddha, which means "Awakened One" or "Enlightened One." His teachings regarding Buddhism have been widely circulated as the philosophy's foundational beliefs.

The Islamic religion has close ties to equanimity as well. The word "Islam" comes from the Arabic word *aslama*, which denotes the peace that comes from total surrender and acceptance. Muslims trace this to God's ultimate wisdom, and many take it to mean that being a Muslim is aligned with being in a state of equanimity.

Equanimity as a spiritual philosophy is one of humanity's deep-seated pillars. It is a spiritual belief that has been taught and praised for centuries. Before delving deeper into the individual elements of equanimity, it's necessary to recognize how it has been woven into society for millennia.

The Elements of Equanimity

It's one thing to say that you should aim for One More level of equanimity. It's quite another to understand how you should get there. Like any challenge, begin by breaking a big concept like equanimity into smaller parts. That will add clarity and simplicity, and make it easier to accept equanimity in its entirety.

As you study equanimity and how it relates to your beliefs and religion, some elements of it may or may not resonate with you. I'm going to give you some overarching principles, but **it's up to you to decide how best to approach your version of equanimity in a way that makes the most sense to you**.

Here are several key points to consider:

- **Equanimity is about finding serenity as you battle the challenges in your life.** You're going to get tossed about. That's life, and there's no hiding from it. While we can't control outside forces, we can be mindful of how we think and react to them.
- This awareness lets us quiet our minds. **Serenity is about accepting there are some things we simply can't change.** Finding serenity requires practice. Meditation toward equanimity requires that you consciously release preferences for or against all things. Your actions are guided

more by your values and virtues instead of your desires that are reactions to positive or negative feelings.

- **Equanimity is about recognizing impermanence.** No matter what is happening in your life right now, it won't last forever. **Life is all about change and impermanence.** When you recognize this, you understand that good times and bad will pass through your life.
- Clinging to the good or the bad can only lead to pain. It's easy to understand how hanging on to the bad creates pain. But recognize that **when you hang on to the good, it can also be a source of pain when it leaves.** Equanimity is about doing away with permanence and the pain associated with it. Equanimity creates a space of awareness that lets every piece of stimulation come and go. **Thoughts are just thoughts. Sounds are only sounds. People are just being themselves. And events are only events.**
- **Equanimity reminds us of our insignificance.** We often place way too much focus on ourselves. **When we're able to come to grips that we're only one small part of the vast human condition, it liberates us from the pressures we place on ourselves.**
- Our fears shrink when we put them into perspective. We don't run from pain or avoid blame or loss with such vigor. We accept our state and work toward balance in our lives with added calmness. **Equanimity is about letting go.** If a challenge or setback in your life is heavy, set it down. Let it go. Learn how to detach from negative beliefs, resentment, pain, and hurt.
- **One of the Four Noble Truths proclaimed by Buddha is that attachment is the origin of suffering.** The attachment to desire or the attachment to desire not to have something both create anxiety and fear. Letting go of both and

accepting what comes into your life, good and bad, release us from a prison of our thoughts.

Ajahn Chah, a twentieth-century Thai Buddhist monk, summarized it well when he said, *"If you let go a little, you will have a little peace. If you let go a lot, you will have a lot of peace. If you let go completely, you will have complete peace."*

- **Equanimity embraces change.** Instead of getting stuck in the status quo, recognize that your future lies in the winds of change. **Acceptance of change, which is inevitable, brings about peace. Fighting change is a waste of time.**

These concepts only scratch the surface of what equanimity is. If you're interested, I strongly encourage you to dig deeper. There are whole libraries on equanimity and how it is a fixture in so many cultures and religions. The more you know about equanimity, the greater your potential for One More level of equanimity in your life.

As part of your further exploration, looking at the Eight Worldly Winds is an excellent place to start.

The Eight Worldly Winds

Buddhism has identified four sets of opposing states that exist in our lives. They are called the Eight Worldly Winds, sometimes known as the Eight Worldly Dharmas. They appear with various labels but are generally accepted as:

- Pleasure and Pain
- Praise and Blame
- Gain and Loss
- Fame and Disgrace

The goal of equanimity is to lessen the effects these winds have on your mind that occur to one extent or the other every day. Examples of the Eight Worldly Winds might be:

- We fall madly in love, only to find out our lover has cheated on us.
- Our success can be exciting, but it could also lead to arrogance.
- We get a big promotion at work, only to have the company declare bankruptcy six months later.
- We root hard for a sports hero or famous musician and then discover they have a severe drug problem, a criminal past, or they unexpectedly pass away, such as Kobe Bryant did.

We must balance good and bad so that while we recognize the good news, we also understand it isn't permanent. **We accept that the world will balance things over time.** In this way, we neither get too high or too low when we react to these events. This isn't to say we shouldn't feel joy or happiness when something good happens. We just need to put it into perspective. Equanimity allows us to do that.

Without equanimity as a governor, going back and forth is exhausting. The goal is complete mental calmness. Sometimes we can reach that state, but since the pursuit of equanimity is a lifelong venture, we must refine our approach and course-correct as we go along.

All Eight Worldly Winds are teachers. From a spiritual point of view, we need all eight in our lives. Without one half of the pair, the other ceases to exist or carries no meaning. However, too much preoccupation with the Eight Worldly Winds is considered a barrier to equanimity. Being too caught up in them creates emotional instability.

Equanimity attempts to steer a course down the middle of each of these pairs. It does not entirely fall in line with one side or the other. Equanimity accepts the reality of each wind without following it. The realization is that the winds are not permanent, and when they change, it's easier to respond with more flexibility.

All of this philosophy is well and good. However, you must decide what your relationship is with equanimity now and in the future.

Your Relationship with Equanimity

When it comes to equanimity, people generally fall into one of four categories.

- Aggressive and with equanimity
- Aggressive and lacking equanimity
- Passive with equanimity
- Passive and lacking equanimity

Of these, there's only one ideal state you should target: Aggressive and with equanimity.

If you're passive, equanimity won't help you much, other than to be a nagging part of your brain that reminds you that you're too laid back and calm to accomplish anything significant in your life. You must bring a certain level of tenacity to your life. You don't have to turn up the dial to "10" at all times, but **you must lead a life where you get stuff done!**

I mentioned at the beginning of this chapter that I haven't always approached life with enough equanimity. I admit that I was such a hard charger that I threw my life out of balance, and I didn't even know it at the time. Sure, I got stuff done. I made a lot of money. But **I paid a higher price than I needed by not practicing equanimity for many years.** The journey to equanimity does not happen overnight. As I learned, it requires years of being mindful and intentional in your thoughts and actions.

One More thinkers also understand equanimity is not permanent. It's fleeting and will come and go as various challenges occur in your life. **You will move between degrees of equanimity from day to day and moment to moment.** My goal is to make sure you don't go through life without enough equanimity as I did. Find peace and mental calmness as soon as you can.

Your relationship with equanimity is the force that makes many other good things possible in life.

18

One More Prayer

*The first gulp from the glass of natural sciences will make you
an atheist, but at the bottom of the glass, God is waiting.*
—*Warner Heisenberg*

CAN YOU SEE FAITH? CAN YOU TOUCH, TASTE,
OR SMELL IT?

Of course not.

But for eons, **faith has remained the single most dominant
and driving force in man's search for spiritual peace
and truth.**

I know that faith is a highly personal choice for everyone.
I respect people of all faiths and the freedom to pursue that

faith in whatever way brings the most meaning to each of you in your own lives. Having said that, I wouldn't be writing a book that's true to myself if I didn't share with you the significant impact my faith as a Christian has had on my life. In fact, it's had the biggest impact of anything on my life.

Quite frankly, I've struggled writing this chapter, not because of the deep belief in my faith, but because I want share with you the huge impact I know prayer can have on your life. I also want to be transparent about my love of Jesus. Having said that, I also want to be respectful of your beliefs and not push you away by preaching.

This is not a chapter about religion. **This is a chapter about using prayer and faith as a strategy to help you achieve your goals.** And even if faith doesn't play a big role in your life, keep reading, because I'm also going to tell you how I think science can't impact your life in this area as well.

That leads us to a fundamental question.

What Is Faith?

We know faith moves mountains, but that only begins to scratch the surface of what faith truly is.

Faith is universal. Every civilization since the beginning of time has practiced some sort of faith-based spirituality.

It's also fair to say that prayer is the manifestation of faith.

Faith and prayer combine to give you paths to peace, truth, conviction, and living by a moral code. They go hand in hand, but each is uniquely different, and they exist in harmony for your benefit.

In One More terms, approach faith as your thoughts. Approach prayers as your actions. When you combine them, they form a bond unlike anything else. That's why it's important to think about your faith often and then act by committing to prayer often, too.

Most people are driven by some form of faith that is strengthened and confirmed by prayers. Prayers strengthen your faith-based beliefs. In turn, that defines your character, what you think about yourself, and how you treat others.

In fact, I can attest that One More Prayer has drawn me closer to Jesus every day of my life.

Consciously and subconsciously, you pray more than you realize. You may not always view it as prayer, but your mind's natural tendency is to think about what you want in life. You see them as desires, but in reality, **desires are a form of prayer**.

When you desire a job promotion, a happy and loving relationship, good health, or wealth, whether you realize it or not, you are engaging in a form of prayer.

That leads to several questions.

Are you praying often enough? Is prayer a regular part of your daily activities? Do you only pray when you need your God's help? How often do you give intentional thought to what it is you pray about? Are you practicing gratitude when you pray and after your prayers are answered?

How Do You Define Faith and Prayer?

Just as every person has a unique relationship with their God, **faith and prayer take on a highly personal meaning for every one of us.**

Consider how the Bible defines faith in Hebrews 11:1, "*Now faith is confidence in what we hope for and assurance about what we do not see.*"

While there are universal truths and beliefs we can all agree on, when it comes to defining faith and prayer, we hold some thoughts based on how we perceive faith, prayer, and our relationship with a higher being.

The presence of faith and the ability to pray are unique to humankind. Our ability to think conceptually above and beyond what we see, touch, and feel in the world separates us from other living beings.

Free will means that we can interpret faith on a personal level. From that interpretation, we can pray on a personal level as well.

Faith has applications beyond those associated with religion. **Faith relies on trust and loyalty to a duty, person, or thing.** And in broad terms, **faith is based on accepting a proposed truth, absent proof of the truth**.

Prayer is more narrowly defined. For many people, the purpose of prayer is to increase our understanding of what our God calls good while also increasing desire in us for what is good.

So, defining faith and prayer essentially means trusting that these things are intended to cultivate the good in us.

Often, people resist embracing faith because they feel like they need to know everything about a particular faith before feeling comfortable doing so. For some of you, that type of thinking not only applies to faith but to all parts of your life.

What do I mean by this?

If you feel you need to reach a certain threshold of knowledge before moving forward with something, you will become paralyzed by inaction and fall behind those who are more willing than you to step into the unknown and act anyway.

To live a full life, there must be several times when you suspend the necessity of needing to know everything before you act. This is especially true with faith because we're never going to know everything there is to know about faith. By its very definition, faith precludes this type of thinking.

Does this limiting thinking hold you back not only in your faith, but also in other areas of your life?

For example, suppose you're the type of person who needs to know everything there is to know before jumping into action. In that case, chances are you're never going to be the person who risks starting their own business or entering a new romantic relationship. **A "need to know everything in advance" belief system will not serve you well throughout your life.**

Every area of our lives, especially faith, depends on stepping into the unknown to some degree or another.

Drawing Strength from My Faith and Prayers

I'm often asked what my favorite book is, and for me, there has always been only one answer.

The Bible.

And my favorite scripture is Philippians 4:13, "*I can do all things through Christ who strengthens me.*"

I am fortified every time I read the Bible. I also have a deep and ongoing curiosity about the nature of humanity, profound spiritual questions, and moral questions that have challenged me to find answers for many years now.

One of the ways I draw strength is through a simple passage that sums up the simplicity and purity of being faithful and praying often.

In John 16:24, Jesus said, "Ask, and you will receive, and your joy will be complete."

That is the essence of faith and prayers and the impact it has had on my life.

More than that, **because I believe fully in the power of faith and prayer, I am never alone.**

Throughout my entire life, I have drawn considerable strength from the positive impact of faith and prayers. That has given me **supreme confidence** every time I walk into a sales call, step on stage at a public speaking event, or when I'm simply out and about, meeting and talking to people on the street.

I have been rewarded through my faith and prayers, too. I firmly believe there is a direct correlation between the wealth I've achieved, the business relationships and friendships I've been blessed with, and most importantly, the ongoing and blissful family life I enjoy.

It's difficult to explain the feeling that faith and prayers have on you to someone who does not practice these things regularly.

I can only give witness to what these things have done for me. I believe, if practiced correctly, **faith and prayers should be used as a time to search for inner peace, to reflect on the nature of your life, and to practice gratitude for the gifts you have been given.**

I draw strength from the calmness that results. This helps center and focus me on what comes next. And from there, I can find purpose and energy when it's time to move forward with the various parts of my life.

Linking Faith, Energy, and Quantum Science

People often ask me if my deep belief in my faith means I can't also believe in science. Absolutely not. Quite the contrary.

There are three philosophies related to the fundamental nature of life as we know it.

1. **Some people consider themselves incredibly faith-based.**
2. **Others think of themselves as energy-based.**
3. **Finally, others are science-based.**

I'm somewhat unique because I consider myself a member of all three camps.

I'm a Christian, but I also believe I have an almighty God who created the universe. I'm a huge believer in science and energy as well. In no way do I think that these doctrines conflict with each other.

At one point, I used to think what I believed about science meant that I had to reduce the depths of my beliefs in my faith. Conversely, I also thought that I had to discount many scientific principles as a way of maintaining my strong faith-based beliefs.

However, as I've read and learned more, I've come to realize that **science has actually confirmed my beliefs in the complexities, beauty, and the marvelous nature of my faith.**

My almighty God, He created everything, or he did not.

The basic definition of quantum science is that the universe is filled with particles that interact with each other and flow with quantum energy. The scientific explanation of this energy is referred to as the study of quantum physics.

What I love about quantum energy is that this is where faith and science intersect. In fact, some of my most devout friends of all faiths, including pastors, rabbis, imams, priests, and others, are very much into the idea of energy.

My belief in these three ideas stems from a probing question I asked myself long ago.

By knowing a God exists who put trees, animals, oceans, gravitational fields, weather, and ALL the other things in our world, why can't that God be the same creator of the energy we all feel and experience in the world?

Despite the enormity of this question, by accepting the premise that energy is felt by all of us and that God is the creator of this energy, that is far less monumental than God creating the complexity of man and woman.

To me, creating an energy field pales in comparison to **giving seven billion people the ability to think, question, express emotions, and challenge, reason, and ponder the great questions of our world**. Most important, He gave us the gift of finding answers to many of those questions, propelling us forward as a civilization since time began.

This is in addition to the biological miracles that give each of us the essence of life. Consider God's miracle of procreation, the transfer of oxygen in our bodies to sustain life, processing food and water into energy, the gifts of sight, sound, taste, and other amazing sensory experiences we use to navigate in the world.

Think about that for a moment.

Truly let the question sink in as to why and how you came to exist.

Not only do I believe faith, energy, and science exist to give us answers, peace, logic, order, and whatever we need in our lives, I know each of these elements exists because I've personally experienced them time and time again.

I've been fascinated for a long time by the unseen energy in our world, how it folds into my faith, and how I pray.

At first glance, it doesn't seem that faith and science have anything in common. However, it may surprise you to learn that **spiritual leaders and scientists have sought ways to link the two for a long time now.**

Quantum physics makes the argument that everything can be broken down into infinitesimal particles and waves, creating unseen energy that drives the universe. Just like faith, quantum-sized particles can't be seen, but scientists and religious scholars operate under the assumption that both have a significant influence on humanity.

One of the basic tenets of quantum physics is the belief that you are creating an answer to a question by making a decision. Faith operates the same way. Additionally, if you had made another decision or used another method, the truth you settled on might have ended up looking very different. Faith leads you to certain answers. Those answers create decisions and outcomes.

Can you see the link of how science and spirituality are connected? Isn't this how faith and prayer guide us to the right decisions?

That interconnectedness helps strengthen the argument for the importance of understanding the unseen energy of faith and the core practice of prayer. The intersection of science and faith has become an increasingly cutting-edge area of study as humanity continues to question the most profound elements of our very existence.

The essence of the link between faith and energy is this.

Many people believe that if they embrace faith and prayer, they must then exclude the concept of energy in the universe. I believe just the opposite is true. Believing in energy and quantum science strengthens my faith and my purposeful prayers. They feed off each other instead of excluding each other.

The more you pray, the more often people will feel your energy, peace, comfort, and empathy. For that reason, regardless of your faith or what you believe, I recommend you pray more often.

You Are Always Making People Feel Something

Have you ever been around someone, and you immediately felt attracted or not attracted to them? I know you will have met several people in your life where you just instantly hit it off with them because of the way they made you feel.

Believe it or not, that's part of quantum physics. That is part of the unseen energy of the world.

That same unseen energy exists in other ways. Would you agree with me that there's an energy force that keeps your feet on the ground, and it's called gravity?

Have you ever walked into a room and felt a peaceful energy while you were there? Conversely, have you ever walked into a place and the energy did not sit well with you? Maybe it scared you or made you feel uncomfortable.

Here's another excellent example. Have you ever noticed how dogs immediately take to some people, but others can't get within 10 feet of them, or they risk getting bitten?

This is a perfect example of how **the energy you emit says certain things about you** as well. Your ability to be intentional and make people feel or not feel certain things is critical in achieving things in your life that you dream about.

Remember this: **You are always making people feel something.**

There is an energy that attracts certain things to your life and an energy that also repels things away from you as well. If you have an absence of understanding of how this energy works, you are creating a considerable disservice to yourself. However, having a good understanding of this concept will serve you well in your life.

The depths to which you decide to explore this energy and quantum physics are entirely up to you. But to deny its existence is to reject something as fundamental as gravity in our world.

My understanding of this energy and how it works has been critical to my success for many years now. I'm also keenly aware that the vast majority of the people I meet are entirely oblivious to the type of energy they emit and how they make people feel. **Your ability to control and harness the energy you put out is critical to how well you function in the world.**

Also, understand that sometimes the energy you need to put out is loving, sometimes intense, and sometimes understanding. This is the other part of using your energy to its fullest advantage.

The Power of One More Prayer

As I've already mentioned but I want to stress again, faith and prayers are highly personal, and I respect every person and how they choose to practice these things.

I'm happy to share what I know and believe, and if these things make sense to you and help you achieve a higher degree of faith and more focused prayers, that will make me happy. I firmly believe that One More Prayer will draw you closer to your personal faith in whatever form that faith is.

Here are some of the additional things I believe about faith and One More Prayer.

- **The stronger your faith is in whatever you believe, the deeper your commitment to your resulting cause will be.** In strategic terms, think of it this way. If you have faith and you pray that you are the right person for a job promotion, or that you deserve to land a big deal because you have faith, you are the right fit to solve another person or company's problem, the harder you're going to work to make that become a reality.

- At times, your faith will waver, and there will be times in your life when you will have questions for your God. You must **ask these questions and test your faith**. Unless you get answers or at least go searching for them, you'll never strengthen your faith. **You must remove doubt as you encounter it.**
- **Don't pray only when it suits you. Pray every day.** Be consistent. Make it every bit the habit that exercising, eating the right foods, or telling your spouse or children that you love them, is for you.
- You've heard the expression, "There are no atheists in a fox hole." Don't wait until you're in a fox hole of your own. **Pray in good times and in bad. Pray with honesty. Pray with intention.** Do not simply go through the motions when you pray, no matter what shape your life is in.
- **Make sure your prayers and your requests are congruent with the will of your God.** This truth is explicitly stated in 1 John 5:14, *"If we ask anything according to his will, he hears us."*
- **Don't pray for harm or ill will upon anyone. It's not acceptable. Ever.**
- I also believe **the power of prayer has a compounding effect on your life**. The longer you build faith and prayer into an essential part of your life, the more impact it will have on you and the people who matter most to you as well.
- Another thing I have learned is that when tragedy strikes, **you may have a crisis of faith**. But I have also learned that is when you need faith and your prayers the most.
- And finally, at times, others will challenge you or ostracize you for your faith and how you pray. They may not stop

long enough to understand your beliefs, or they may generalize based on their own beliefs and quite possibly their own shortcomings. My response to people like that is that **your relationship with your God is more important than what people think they know and assume about you**.

If you can place your God first, then you are well on your way to effectively incorporating faith and the power of One More Prayer into your life.

19

One Last One More

I'VE HAD MANY EPIPHANIES SINCE I STARTED WRITING *THE POWER OF ONE MORE*. However, one of them stands above all the others.

I realized my life and business philosophy comes from my relationship with my hero and my father, Edward Joseph Mylett, Jr.

My belief that people can change, and the reason I'm in the field of helping people do better in life is because the man I love and looked to above all others did just that.

Although I've shared several things with you, none is more essential or difficult for me to write about than One Last One More. When you watch the person you're closest to in life live a certain way and then commit to a profound change when faced with One Last One More, it not only changes them, it changes you, too.

Over the course of his lifetime, this is the story of how my father taught me one of life's most priceless lessons.

I know you'll find value in it, too.

■ ■ ■

The lesson of One Last One More begins here.

My father was a banker by profession, a hard-working man who never missed a day at work.

He was also an alcoholic for the first 15 years of my life.

He paid a horrible price as he suffered through this disease. And by extension, the people he loved paid a steep price, too.

We became the collateral damage in a war that raged inside of him. Although we had a very loving family, his illness created anxiety and worry in all of us. It was tough to watch my father struggle every day with something I knew he wanted to rid from himself.

But, ironically, I will tell you his drinking happened for me and not to me.

Even more so, my father's alcoholism happened for him and not to him. That's because, through his illness, my father eventually found his true calling in life.

His drinking happened for me because most of the skills I use to this day are because I was raised by an alcoholic father.

For example, I learned to read body language, tonality, and facial expressions as a young boy. I first developed it by learning how to read which father would come home from work. Would it be a sober and loving father or an intoxicated and detached father?

I got to a point where I could figure this out by how my dad would insert a key into our front door lock. If he struggled and fumbled to get the key in the lock, I knew he had been drinking. Conversely, when the key slid into the lock without hesitation, I knew what that meant as well.

Once inside, I paid attention to how he talked and walked, his body language, demeanor, and attitude. It was always a guessing game as to whether I would avoid him until he went to bed or would I get to go out and play catch with him in the backyard.

When you're 8 years old, and this is a skill you need to have for a better home life, you learn that lesson quickly, and you learn it well.

Although deep down my father was a kind-hearted man, when he was drinking, his actions didn't always align with this character. Many times, he was not only emotionally removed from the rest of us, but he was physically removed from time to time as well. There were days and nights when he wouldn't come home, and we all knew the reason why.

Despite this affliction, my father was my best friend, and I looked up to him. He was my hero, confidant, advisor, and the person I trusted above all others. He made me and my three sisters feel special, and we all thought about him in the same way.

Despite challenges in your own families, I know many of you have experienced the things my sisters and I did.

As a young boy, every son starts out thinking his father is perfect . . . someone who can do no wrong. Unfortunately, the nature of life is that a father is human, and he will make mistakes along the way. As a father now, I certainly know I've made them.

But when you're a young boy, and if you're like I was, you stand in awe of your father. You gladly make him your hero, and you look beyond those mistakes and imperfections.

However, I didn't look up to him because I thought he was perfect. In fact, just the opposite was true. It was his ability to overcome his mistakes and shortcomings that made him even more extraordinary in my eyes.

I'll never know exactly why my dad turned to drinking, and I don't think any of us ever figured out why it became an addiction for him.

■ ■ ■

Difficult, challenging, and tragic things happen to everyone, which means there will come a time in your life when these things happen to you. Like it or not, the clock will run out, and no amount of praying, wishing, or begging will deny this inevitability.

One of the immutable laws of the universe is that everything comes with an expiration date.

Let that sink in for a moment.

Sooner or later, everything ends.

No matter who you are or what you're going through, change will come to you. This is not meant to depress you. It's meant to create a sense of urgency in you. It is also to remind you that things are happening for you and not to you.

At several times in your life, you'll reach the end of a journey, and you'll come face to face with One Last One More. In these times, you'll make choices that define your character and change the course of your life.

Your world changes when you realize your days on Earth are finite. Many people come to this realization earlier than others, and some are acutely aware of it but can't break free from those heavy chains they've forged.

At some point, we're all bound together by One Last One Mores. We can't run from them. So, we must learn to face them the best possible way.

Learn to live your life the best way you know how *before* those days come.

You can't stop or slow down the march of time and those inevitable changes. All you can do is make the most of what you have right now. In this way, you can intentionally guide your fate. It's how you can live life with fewer burdens, regrets, anger, and sadness.

And, yes, it's not easy.

Change rarely is.

■ ■ ■

When I was 15, my dad was confronted with the biggest One Last One More of his life: My mother gave him an ultimatum.

"Either you get sober or lose your family. You won't get another chance," she told him.

I'll never forget what my dad said to me when faced with this.

"Eddie, I'm going to go away for a while, and I'm going to stop drinking. When I come back, you're going to have the father you deserve. Your sisters are going to have the dad they deserve. And your mother is going to have a husband worthy of her."

I had heard this before, and I wanted desperately to believe him. So, I asked him, "How is this time going to be any different?"

I'd never seen my dad cry before, but that day, with tears in his eyes, he said, "I have One More chance, Eddie."

One Last One More.

My father, who struggled with his addiction and tried to get sober many times before, took those words to heart. The stakes were now so high that one more failure was no longer an option.

Here's the lesson I took from that and want to share with you.

Linking huge emotional reasons to what you want to accomplish is the key to why you must be willing to go through the difficult struggles associated with change.

Those reasons to change must be overwhelmingly more significant than the obstacles you face so that those obstacles are dwarfed in comparison. If you show me somebody with big enough reasons to change in their life, I'll show you somebody capable of making that change.

I'm often asked where you can find those reasons.

You need to look no further than your dreams or the people in your life.

For my father, the tough challenge of getting and staying sober was nowhere near as significant as the reason to change, which was the catastrophic possibility of losing his family. To him, as a devoted and loving family man, there was no more significant loss than taking his family away from him.

Until that time, my father was a man who had not lived up to a life he was capable of living.

He knew it. He also knew he had to change. And he did.

■ ■ ■

My father didn't go looking for redemption when he got sober. But that's exactly what he found.

Part of that redemption is revealed on the pages of this book. Although I'm writing it, the things you've read about are a shared legacy with him.

I'm often asked how I got into the business of helping others.

It wasn't by accident. It was because of my father.

The Power of One More is a direct result of my father's influence on me. My desire to help others reflects my father's determination to devote his life to helping others after he got sober.

Through his work with Alcoholics Anonymous, my father embraced the idea of living One More day sober, a core mantra of AA. In fact, it became the entire premise of his life.

That may sound like a small thing to overcome if you've never battled addiction. But in the world of an alcoholic, winning this fight One More day at a time means everything.

Once he committed to it, my dad didn't try to stay sober every remaining day of his life. He tried to stay sober One More day of his life. One day at a time, stacked upon each other until days became weeks and months, and they became years. The difference in that kind of mindset means everything to a recovering alcoholic.

If you're reading this and you're thinking about quitting on your dream, a business you've started, or anything important to you, don't put the pressure on yourself to meet that goal for five or ten years, or the rest of your life. Instead, think about not quitting for One More day.

Take things One More small step at a time. Make your goal of not quitting manageable and easier to achieve. All you need to do is get through today. Tomorrow, you can start again and conquer your battles with a One Last One More mentality.

In your darkest and most challenging times, I know many of you think about quitting and giving up. When those thoughts occur to you, just hold on for One More day.

Don't quit for One More day.

As I mentioned, for the longest time, I didn't fully realize the entire premise of my life came from my father, his attempts to get sober, and his belief in One Last One More. But that's exactly how he lived the final 35 years of his life.

It bears repeating because One Last One More is *the* lesson of this book.

■ ■ ■

My dad had suffered from chronic obstructive pulmonary disease (COPD) for several years but still managed to get around well most of the time. And then, one day he started laboring heavily during one of our golf rounds.

A month later, he was diagnosed with liposarcoma, a rare type of cancer that develops in fatty tissues and can grow anywhere in your body. Shortly after that, my dad underwent a 12-hour surgery to remove a tumor the size of a football in his chest.

He never complained through the surgeries, chemotherapy, radiation, medications, and other treatments that followed. He hid the severity of his illness from us, knowing we would be upset if we knew how much he was suffering.

My father battled his cancer for nine long years before passing away from related respiratory complications on October 30, 2020, less than a year ago as I write this. He was 72 years old.

There is a crushing void in my life where he used to be. I miss him like no other and I still struggle with not having him around. I long for our conversations and the time we spent together.

While I expect the hole where he was in my life to get smaller over time, deep down, I know I'll continue to miss him every day I remain on this Earth.

The magic of time is that it allows us to heal and reflect, and that's precisely what I've done since my father's passing. It's an ongoing process, but I've been able to put some perspective on his life and how all of us can take away important lessons from who Edward Joseph Mylett, Jr. was and who he continues to be.

■ ■ ■

There are three things I want you to know about One Last One More:

1. **Live a One Last One More life as often as you can.**
2. **One Last One More works best when you treat every day as a new life.**
3. **Understand that it's never too late for One Last One More.**

■ ■ ■

When you live a One Last One More life as often as you can, you approach life with a high degree of urgency.

What if you were only allowed One Last One More dance with the person you love? What if you could only have One Last One More conversation with your children? What would you say to them, and how would you say it? Think about your life if you only had One Last One More chance to tell your spouse that you love them.

Consider how you would act if, like my father, you were given One Last One More chance to be the parent, the sibling, the child, or the friend you always wanted to be? When you approach life with a One Last One More mentality, your priorities become clear. You are more grateful for God's gifts that have been given to you. You respect and appreciate time.

And you will become a better human being.

Here's the best example I can tell you of how One Last One More impacted my relationship with my dad.

My father and I loved to play golf. When I was a young man, we would play rounds at El Prado Golf Course in Chino, California. For us, it became our haven, a place where we could go to unwind, laugh, and share our thoughts and problems with each other.

We had lively discussions about politics all the time. We also talked about spirituality, the meaning of life, and about his children and grandchildren. In our quieter moments, he'd reflect on some of the regrets in his life, mainly about the chances he didn't take.

Although he was proud of me, my dad always stressed that while my business success was beyond admirable, he made sure

I understood my relationships with my family and friends are what mattered most. He cared little about the houses I owned, my wealth, and the other trappings of success. Instead, he was more concerned about the man I was, how I treated people, what difference I was making in the world, and whether I was living a good and virtuous life.

What he valued remains one of the most important lessons he ever taught me. It has kept me grounded to this day.

Our talks were deep, and over the years, he became the only person who knew everything about me. Even as I approached 50 years old, he was the first person I called for advice. In fact, my dad was the *only* person I ever called for advice. He was also the first person I called whenever something happened, good or bad.

As my career took off and I started to enjoy a measure of success, I wanted to give my dad the gift of playing one of the finest golf courses in the world.

So, around the Christmas holidays for many years, the two of us would travel to Pebble Beach for an annual father and son golf getaway. It was a small measure of thanks for all he had given me, and those times are among the most meaningful moments of my life.

Whether it was playing at El Prado or Pebble Beach, these trips were not so much about golf as they were about spending time together. It could have just as easily been about going fishing, turning wrenches on a classic car, taking in a ball game, or whatever common interests fathers and sons enjoy together.

Although I had grown into a man, I needed my dad as much as ever. As a father with my own challenges, my dad provided wise counsel and a place I could go for life advice, as only a father can.

I miss so many things about my dad, but I miss these golf outings the most. I always had a sense of how important they were, but now that my father is gone, they've taken on a new level of meaning. Make no mistake, it's not the golf I miss. It's the hours I spent with him, just sharing time.

I would give anything for One Last One More round of golf with my dad.

■ ■ ■

Many times, I still can't believe he's gone.

Months after he passed, I spoke to an audience of several thousand people, and I couldn't wait to get off the stage to call my dad. Like past conversations, I was excited to go over what went well and what I could have done better.

It wasn't until the adrenaline left my body and I was standing backstage by myself that I realized I couldn't do that any longer.

I can't tell you how many times I've had that same initial rush and awkward feeling since my dad's passing. But I can tell you with certainty that the clarity of what One Last One More means in all parts of my life has never been greater.

If you take nothing else away from this book, I'm telling you now, if you have someone in your life who means a lot to you, start living your life with a One Last One More mentality toward them. Cherish every moment you spend together and live your life in ways that will make them proud and make you happy.

Don't wait!

My father would be embarrassed if he thought this book was about him. For his sake, and mine, it's not. This book is about you and your families, your soul, your relationships with others, and the legacies you're creating.

I'm only using my relationship with my father to help you understand why living a One Last One More life is the urgent frame of mind you need to live your best life.

■ ■ ■

The second thing I want you to understand is that to fully appreciate One Last One More, treat every day as a new life.

There are no guarantees.

You or someone you care about can be here one moment and gone the next.

You are blessed every second you're alive, and you need to approach those moments with extreme gratitude. Learn to appreciate things, big and small, and the people God has brought into your life.

Release the thoughts and people that weigh you down. When you let these things go, you'll replace them with opportunities and relationships that were meant for you. Your priorities will change as you cast off the past. Too many people get stuck in the quicksand of their memories, and they drown needlessly in guilt, anger, and stupid grudges that only hurt themselves.

Instead, when you wake up in the morning, tell yourself this: **"Every day I am alive, I am reborn."**

When you let go of your past, you create space for the here and now. You can bring energy and enthusiasm to the fleeting nature of One Last One Mores into your life. You can direct your energy to what matters, and not things that will destroy your inner well-being and your relationships with others.

When you treat every day as a new life, you'll find more enjoyment and bliss in the things that serve you well. If you must have a One Last One More conversation with someone, one last hug before a goodbye, or one last dance before someone you care about goes away, you can do so with a clear mind, free from the mental garbage that gets in the way of living your best life.

Don't spoil today by lugging that garbage around. Instead, toss it away and get on with the things that matter.

■ ■ ■

The third and final thing to know is that it's never too late for One Last One More.

After my father died, I came across several index cards as I was putting away some of his things. On these cards were scribbled codes like "1-4, JL" and "1-3, PT." They were scattered on his vanity unit and taped to his bathroom mirror. These codes were dates and the initials of someone's name, and there were hundreds of them.

I soon figured out that every one of those cards represented a person my dad had helped get sober, and the dates were that person's sobriety anniversary date.

Here's the most remarkable part. On those dates, my father would call that person, wish them a happy sobriety birthday, and congratulate them. His message to them was simple. All you must do is stay sober for ONE MORE DAY.

He made these calls hundreds of times a year. Every year. Including in the last days of his life.

Even while he was on oxygen, struggling to breathe, and could barely whisper, he still reached out and made calls to the people on his notecards. Although he was in severe pain and agony, and he knew he would pass away soon, my father had to help one more person.

Nobody was watching. Nobody would have known whether he made those calls or not. However, because my father lived a One More life, this was an opportunity for him to help One Last One More human being. In the end, my father's One Last One More was a phone call to another person in need shortly before he passed away.

I've never been so moved or prouder of my dad. His quiet, kind, and humble gestures remain a profound example of service to others that I may never match.

Now you know why I've made it my sincere mission to try and help as many people as possible in my life, too.

I do it to honor my father.

Coming back from the brink of losing his family and everything he worked for, my father found purpose and redemption. He made the most of the One Last One More chance he was given. Our physical being dies, and we do pass from this Earth at some point. But my father's One Last One More legacy will live through the ages.

We should all be so lucky to live our lives that well.

■ ■ ■

God, in His infinite wisdom, gave us the power of forgiveness. Take this gift to heart. If you have a challenging relationship with someone you care about, find a way to set your differences aside.

You simply don't know what comes next.

When you find it in your heart to make One Last One More a priority in your life, not only will you lighten the chains of another person, but you'll lighten your chains in life as well.

As I watched my father take his final breaths, it dawned on me that one day, we'll all face our One Last One More.

Our last year on Earth.

Our last month, last week, and our last day.

Our last hour.

And all too soon, our final breath.

You can't control the end, but you can control the story in between.

Your ability to live your best life is going to be shaped, in large part, by the One Mores I've revealed to you in this book. These thoughts and actions will build the story of your life so that when you do take that one last breath, you can be proud of the life you've lived.

Don't wait for One Last One Mores to find you.

Go after them with urgency and purpose.

You'll unlock the most difficult and essential One More lesson you can learn when you do this.

And in doing so, you may just unlock the secret to life itself.

About the Author

Ed Mylett is a highly successful entrepreneur who has blended his unique experiences with a diverse set of practical strategies that have made him one of the most sought-after inspirational speakers in the world today.

As a young man, he attended the University of the Pacific in Stockton, California, where he was a three-time academic All-American before an untimely injury ended his dream of playing in the major leagues.

At his father's urging, Ed became a counselor for disadvantaged children in what turned out to be one of the pivotal turning points of his life. It was there he first started to appreciate the importance of serving others and laying the foundation for success principles he would put into practice later in life.

Ed is a serial entrepreneur who has enjoyed considerable success in part through his unrivaled work ethic and ability to fire up people with his dynamic, high-octane presentations. Over the years, he has been involved in several tech, real estate, medical, and food ventures, among many others, leading him to be named a *Success Magazine* SUCCESS 125 most influential leader in 2022.

With a strong desire to help people, Ed began sharing his inspirational and performance strategies live and online. In four short years, he amassed more than two million Instagram followers, wrote a best-selling book, and launched a popular weekly podcast, *The Ed Mylett Show*. Ed thoroughly enjoys engaging with his followers and is active on several social media platforms where his posts are viewed several million times each month.

As a keynote speaker, Ed has spoken to millions of people. He is equally adept at delivering relatable strategies in intimate gatherings, to arenas filled with 50,000 people, or online to audiences in the hundreds of thousands.

He is well known for combining spirituality, faith, the inner workings of the mind, and tactical thoughts and actions to help people produce real changes in their lives.

Ed remains humble about his success, attributing his good fortune to his faith in God, his mentors, and the lessons his father taught him throughout life.

In his free time, Ed is an avid golfer, health, and weightlifting enthusiast. He and his wife Kristianna are the proud parents of two adult children.